AUTOBIOGR
'LIFE OF A LON
By H.T. Ben

GW01048765

If procrastination is to put somet
then I am guilty of this. Looking b
a Depot and Traffic Manager in C
day various representatives would call in for a coffee and a
chat and we would reminisce about our yesterdays. One day
one of the reps said to me, 'Harry, you should put your story
down on paper, you have led an interesting life, it would
make a great book!' So here I am.

My name is Henry Thomas Benton, born 22 May 1931 in
Camberwell, South East London. My early years were spent
in a slum, but during 1935 we moved to a council flat in East
Dulwich.

Over the years I have seen many things, but one of the
most memorable events that I have witnessed was the night
that my sisters and I watched Crystal Palace burn. During the
Blitz our flat was flattened to the ground and 4 years later a
flying bomb hit our local hospital, the blast blowing me 15 to
18 feet into a main road. As sweets were rationed and money
was in short supply, I set up a little stall and sold home-made
toffee apples, and firewood made from chopped up bomb
damaged doors.

I have met many different people in my life, including,
Matt Monro, Dennis Lotus, Miss Great Britain, and His Royal
Highness Prince Faisal of Saudi Arabia. Not forgetting the
Mayor of Miami who bought me dinner in Scotland, and the
Key and Freedom of the City of Miami. Also I was a stand in
for Michael Caine on the film set for 'Top Deck'.

I have led an interesting and sometimes colourful life,
from being asked to drive a vehicle on the Great Train
Robbery – an offer which fortunately I did not take up - to
being dubbed 'The French Letter Man' for selling
contraception to canteen staff at Shannon Airport.

Publisher's Name and Address
Henry Thomas Benton
PO Box 30
Kent
DA3 7BU

ISBN 0-9540826-0-5
Edited and typed by Jennifer Paton

Acknowledgement list of ILLUSTRATIONS that can be seen on the rear pages and front cover.

Front cover   Myself promoting London and the UK 1969.

a)   Dad having a pint in the 'Cherry Tree' in Grove Vale, East Dulwich, South London.

b)   Vehicle that has crippled me for over 50 years.

c)   Two headhunters from Borneo, Dyaks or Dayaks, I am 'piggy in the middle'.

d)   Having a drink with Ken Lockobie on Island Penang, Malaya, 1951.

e)   Banfield drivers (not milkmen).   Myself, Patsy and Mac.

f)   Telegram 'Top Deck' film with Michael Caine, I bought his breakfast, 1962.

g)   Miss Great Britain, Joy Black, 2nd on Hughie Green's left - in white swimsuit.

h)   Betty, 2 friends and I at Butlins 1963.

i)   Mayor Jay Dermer handed me the Key and Card of Courtesies for the City of Miami.

j)   Last Cartan tour of Ireland and UK 1969. I am the one holding the board.

Kind courtesies for the extract regarding The Comet comes with permission from RAF Priory, Stanmore, Middlesex.

ISBN 0-9540826-0-5
Edited and typed by Jennifer Paton

PAINT A PICTURE
THE PICTURE WILL GIVE YOU WORDS
FOR A STORY
WHEN HARRY MET KATE

The BENTONs all lived in Southwark, just south of London Bridge, and off the Borough High Street, a little court known as St Margaret Court. It is easy to find, from south to north just walk towards London Bridge and up the Borough High Street, on your left you will see a statue of a soldier from the First World War, here is the passage that leads you into St Margaret Court. Other sights you will see; on the other side of this High Street is the George Inn, this was the site of the old Tabard Inn from which the Canterbury Pilgrims set out, as described by Chaucer; also in this area was the Marshalsea Gaol; and of course Southwark Cathedral which is a must to visit.

The Bentons were costermongers, a costermonger being a person who sells fruit and vegetables from a barrow, and the family was lucky, as nearby was the Borough Market. My Dad had 2 brothers and 5 sisters, however I only know of his brothers. Johnny Benton lived in Dulwich and Sammy Benton I met in 1954 working in a sweet factory near Mitcham Common.

The GARDENERs came from Balham, SouthWest London, but moved to the Elephant and Castle some years later. My Mum was the eldest and had 4 younger sisters to look after, Sophie, Anne, Sally and Florence. Times were hard in those days; Mum would push the barrow to market, fill it up, return home, and then have to get her sisters ready for school. Granddad Gardener died at a young age and Grandma did not remarry.

Whilst in the vicinity of London Bridge, walk across to the City side. On your right you will have a good view of Tower Bridge, and on arriving at the north bank you will see the Great Fire Monument of 1666. One year earlier than that in 1665 was the Great Plague of London when nearly a fifth of the inhabitants of London were lost. Then, in 1666 a

1

baker's shop in Pudding Lane caught fire, causing damage, which in those days was valued at £10 million. 13000 houses, old St Paul's Cathedral, 86 churches and many other civic buildings were lost, but not a great loss of life. Macaulay the Historian said, '**With the permission of heaven, hell broke loose**', meaning that the fire got rid of the black rats which spread the disease.

Cross to the other side of the road and you will see the Fishmongers Hall with ghostly stone figures of fishermen and fish-maids on the riverfront. The Fishmongers was incorporated during the time of Edward I, and bears the statue of the brave Sir William Walworth, Lord Mayor of London, who slew the rebellious Wat Tyler, and the dagger he used is also shown.

London Bridge is the richest bridge in the world. Why? The City Guilds, closely connected with the Government of the city, are Livery Companies or Guilds, of which there were 81 of these companies during the time I was a Registered London Tourist Guide in the sixties. These companies are very wealthy and have devoted large sums for educational and charitable purposes. Each year an amount of money is put into a kitty, like a fund, to build a new London Bridge, so that in years to come the people will not have to pay for a new bridge, therefore it is the RICHEST BRIDGE IN THE WORLD.

The War between the UK and Germany was ready for the kick off. Dad went to the recruiting depot and the soldier said to him, 'What way could you help in this war, Benton?' Dad replied, 'I like riding horses,' and so he was put into the Royal Horse Artillery.

After a few weeks of training, Dad and the regiment were sent to France.

The weather was not too kind to them, Dad said, 'Mud up to your arm pits.' The horses *did* work hard pulling the gun and carriage through the mud to get to the front line, and like in any conflict Dad had his sleep and food where and when he could. Things were rough stuff all around them. After a while Dad became the leading horseman, but he was blown off his horse and received facial damage, a scar from his ear towards his mouth. Dad was in hospital for about 5 weeks and then went back to full duties at the front line. Things were not going good for the Germans, so they dropped gas on our troops. Dad was one of the troopers that was gassed, so back to the hospital again, and when he could breath all right his regiment sent Dad home.

On his return home he helped to train new recruits. Lets put things right, here is a man who was a boxer and could go 10 rounds with chaps heavier than himself and still give them a good fight. Yes, stand toe to toe and fight it out. But now we have a man who can merely walk 100 yards and have to stop for his breath, and over the years I watched Dad get worse. In the end, I would pick Dad up out of his bed and sit him by an open window fanning him, like a boxer, with a towel. But in these early days Dad did not like people to see him in a bad way, so he would turn away and take deep breaths and try not to show it.

Dad met Mum around the Borough Market, had a chat and a cup of tea and told her his name was 'Henry Thomas Benton, but my friends call me Harry Boy.' Mum told Dad, 'My name is Kate short for Catherine,' and so the courting started. My sister Ellen said Mum was going out with another chap at that time, who liked her a lot, but Dad won the day and they were married in St George's Church in the Borough High Street in 1919.

Mum and Dad lived with the Bentons in St Margarets Court.

My Dad worked at Barclay and Perkins Brewery in Southwark on a 5 day week. At weekends Dad would hire a horse and cart to do a fish round, 10 hours on a Saturday and only Sunday mornings. Dad worked at this Brewery for over 21 years, whilst Mum called on Granny Gardener to help her with her sisters. Sophie met and married into the Pettifor family, the Pettifors had horses and stables.

On 11 January 1924, my sister Ellen was born in Edward and Alexandra Hospital, York Road, between Westminster and Waterloo Bridges opposite County Hall, which is now private apartments. So Mum and Dad moved to the Camberwell area, just off Wyndham Road, a tiny street named Bailey Street. Numbers 1 and 2 were lived in by the Pettifors and between 1 and 2 was a gateway leading into the stables. Mum and Dad had just the 1 room to live, eat and sleep in, 1 cold water tap, and a toilet. This toilet was used by all, including visitors to collect the horses. The whole yard was full of cobblestones. Mum would shout at me, 'Do not touch that,' 'that' being horses pooh and large puddles of urine, it was not very nice. Our 1 room was over the gateway.

In 1929 my other sister Kath was born in Kings College Hospital not far away. Things were getting a little bit tight moving around that one room. Mum started work at the Brewery in Southwark, this helped with the cash flow, and then I created another problem 2 years later. Yes, I was born on 22 May 1931, Camberwell, and now there were 5 to move around this one room.

What else do I remember about Bailey Street? Entertainment. I was always looking forward to our Saturday morning Picture Show, the Penny Rush. Flash Gordon and the air space ships, Dr Ming, the Cavemen and the cartoons. This was good!

Saturday night and Sunday lunchtime was punch up time for Mum and Dad. It hurts me to write about this, but it is true, this went on for years and years. As a little boy I cried to my Mum, 'Please Mummy don't keep fighting with Dad, I don't like it.' Mum would say, 'It will not happen again,' but the next weekend just the same.

In Wyndham Road was a Dairy that sold milk on rounds and for the locals who finished late at work. This Dairy had the old brass cow, you put your pint jug under the tit, put in half a penny, turned a brass handle and your jug filled with milk. All the snotty nose kids would be catching the drips of milk; I was one of them.

My sister Ellen carried water buckets up the stairs and had to look after my sister Kath and I. One day Dad said, 'Harry Boy, come on son, we are off to Dulwich.' So we jumped on the tram and rode to East Dulwich, and viewed 14 Goldwell House, in Quorn Road, it was a palace compared to Bailey Street.

In 1935 we moved from the slums to our palace, Dad just loaded the cart and off we went to arrive at 14 Goldwell House, Quorn Road, East Dulwich, SouthEast London. My sisters and I helped to move the so-called furniture into our palace. This was great for Dad, no stairs, a ground floor flat, 2 bedrooms, living room, kitchen, and bathroom with a toilet. In the kitchen was a geezer; this is not an old man, but a pump that we could pump hot water into our bath. It took Mum and Dad 3 minutes to find the local public house, the Cherry Tree; about 3 minutes walk from one house to another house.

The kids in the square were good to us, but for one, Billy the Bully. If my sister was not around he would come up and punch me.

One day I wanted to go indoors, walked to our doorway and he said to me, 'You going indoors Benton?'

'Yes.'

'No you not,' and with that he punched me hard.

I walked away from him and his pals, and up the stairs of our block to the third floor, saw an empty milk bottle, picked it up, looked over the balcony and there was the bully right beneath me. I took aim and dropped the bottle, which smashed within inches of him. Then shouted at the top of my voice, 'The next time you punch me I will not fishing miss you.' I walked down the stairs, gave him a dirty look and went indoors.

*****

Then came the night to remember, 30 November 1936, the last day of autumn. We were running around the square, loosing all track of time, when some other kids came running into our square shouting, 'Fire! Fire! Fire!'

We shouted back, 'Where is this fire?'

'Go to the top of Doggy,' one kid shouted, Doggy being short for Dog Kennel Hill.

So we all ran up the steep hill of Doggy, I was standing next to my 2 sisters watching the People's Palace die, the whole sky was alight like a 1000 search lights.

So, as I was a London Tourist Registered Guide I will now give you my brief history of Crystal Palace, the People's Palace.

The Crystal Palace that burnt down on 30 November 1936 came from the Great Exhibition of London in 1851, but we first turn the clock back to 1850. Queen Victoria summoned the builders of the Government and said that there was to be an Exhibition, which would be built in Hyde Park. It was to be open for just 6 months, starting 1 May 1851 and closing on 31 October 1851. It would house the world's new technology and arts and crafts. The Government then sent out to all the builders to get their plans for the best building to be had.

The Duke of Devonshire's head gardener won the day with his plans. His building would be made from cast iron, timber and glass, mostly glass to bring in the daylight. So work started and finished well on time. His name was J Paxton.

On 1 May 1851 Queen Victoria opened the Great Exhibition. Kings and Queens came from all over the world, as well as other top people like Dukes and Earls. Then it was thrown open to the general public, 6 million people in total visited. This made a great deal of cash and because of this we now have Exhibition Road with the 3 museums, Victoria and Albert, Natural History and the Science, plus the Royal Colleges of Art and Music. This was the start of the building of Kensington, the Royal Borough.

A new company was then formed called The Crystal Palace. The entire building, including the glass, was taken to

6

its new site at Sydenham Hill in South London. It was bigger than the site in Hyde Park standing at 168 feet high and could be seen from many parts of southern England.

On 10 June 1854 the Crystal Palace was opened by Queen Victoria, it housed art, plants, statues and fountains, playing courts, Concert Hall, theatre and an auditorium that could seat 20000. Outside were placed Prehistoric animals which thrilled the kids - some kids ran away from them, but Mum would say, 'It's all right it's not your Dad, the animal is better looking!' – plus motor racing and many other outdoor games.

How did the fire start? The Palace had underfloor heating steam pipes, and the floor was timber. Did someone drop a fag or a cigar end on the floor? And was the wood crispy and ready to light up? No one knows for sure. Fire engines from all over SouthEast London rushed to the scene, the fire was even seen in the English Channel. It started at about 7.30 pm. We were watching until 10 pm when Mum dragged us home, but it burned away all night. When the workers turned up the next day they were told, 'No job, it's all gone.'

And that was the end of the Crystal Palace.

Edward VIII abdicated the throne to marry Wallis Simpson the American divorcee and was thus created the Duke of Windsor. The Duke of York, became King George VI, and his wife Elizabeth was crowned Queen, who we know today as the Queen Mum. In 1937, we the kids had a great day – the Square's party, all the flags, and I remember my china mug with the painted pictures of the King and Queen.

In 1938, Oswarld Mosley, the founder of the British Fascists in 1932, and his men wore brown shirts with armbands and were marching up and down Doggy and round to Peckham Rye Park. They stood on rostrums giving speeches about a country called Germany, its people and what good work they were doing.

I spoke to my Dad and said, 'What is all that about Dad?'

'It could be another war, this bloke Hitler is invading other countries and if it goes on someone must stop him.'

1939 - 1945
SECOND WORLD WAR

On 3 September 1939 war was declared on Germany. Neville Chamberlain was Prime Minister, 1937 to 1940, although he pursued a policy of appeasement towards Germany following the German invasion of Poland.

Mum said, 'I will send you away, it will be safer for you.'

There I was in 1940, standing outside East Dulwich railway station with a gas mask, sandwich and some fruit. I was told, 'You are going a long way to miss the bombs that could soon be dropping.' Now this long way was in fact to North Holmwood near Dorking, a mere 24 miles away. We did have the bombs dropping and the dog fights so what was the point of this train ride?

North Holmwood is a lovely village. As you drive in from Dorking, on your right are a few shops and a few yards up is the village school. On your left is the village pond and houses lay back off the village green with the old village church. I was in the choir of this church and went to that village school.

One day they removed my tonsils following some problems, but my Mum did not come to visit me. The Blitz of London had started on 7 September 1940 and our flat at 14 Goldwell House was bombed on the 15 September just one week on, so my family was homeless. They would stay one night here and one night there until a house was free at 1 Constance Road, right across from Quorn Road.

Mum brought me back home, so now I am looking for work. I went to the local paper shop where the owner gave me 2 paper rounds. In the mornings I would go to St Francis Hospital where I would sell fags, papers and matches to the very old and sick people. I would then buy 6d of cakes from the bakers in Grove Vale and eat some on the way to school, saving the others for my lunch. At night I would do a paper round around Dulwich village, the big houses, including Pond House. In the summer I would ask the owners of these houses if I could pick up the windfalls from their fruit trees,

8

and was told I could. I did just that and when I saw my Mum asked her for more sugar and jam. I was going to make toffee apples!

Mum was good at asking for things that were hard to come by, and so now I had what I needed including a small saucepan but still needed small wooden stakes to stick into the toffee apples. I sat there thinking. Yes! Yes! The bombed houses, their damaged doors, so away I went to search. Just the other side of Doggy is Champion Hill and a few yards down on the other side were much damaged houses on a bombsite. I understood that a landmine had hit this spot. I pulled my little home-made cart and chopped up the stakes. Whilst doing this more thoughts came into my head. Don't stop at toffee apples, prepare for the coming winter and sell bowls of firewood. So when the winter came I was still able to make a few pennies.

My mates were Johnny Evendon, Johnny and George Clement, Eddie Todd and, I must use a Biblical name here, Moses (later in the book you will understand why), to name but a few. We all pulled the girls, the best one I ever pulled was Carol Curtess who lived up Quorn Road. Carol was a top girl, good looks and very kind with it.

On one occasion Johnny Evendon did this to me. 'Hi Harry, I got a good looking girl for you, if you are up for it?' Me, dopey nut, fell for it again. Two young ladies turned up, his one being just the right size, but my one was 6 feet tall, I didn't even come up to her arm pits. He'd done it again, put one over on me!

On 12 July 1944 I was kicking a ball about in Constance Road just outside my house when **I could suddenly hear the drone of a flying bomb. This one was not that far away and then the engine cut out, the droning noise stopped and this is when everyone in the area should run for their lives. I was petrified and just looked up. The flying bomb was coming over the roof tops of the flats, dropping all the time, just like an aeroplane coming in to land,** over the top of the small houses in Constance Road, missing the trees in the road and over into the St Francis Hospital area. There

9

was in a split second an almighty explosion, all the windows were blown out of the houses in the road and I could hear the glass smashing. With that I was lifted up and thrown about 15 to 18 feet towards the bottom of Doggy. I was in a bad way, blood running down my nose, ears ringing, I could hardly breath and my chest was hurting. I crawled to the kerb where I sat and cuffed the blood from my nose. I was in pain and had a bad headache. I waited a while and then went to the pub to tell Mum and Dad the story of the flying bomb. All that Dad said was, 'You caught the blast of the bomb then.'

It took a few days for me to get better as I suffered with headaches.

After the incident with the flying bomb I was informed that I was lucky to be alive, I still did my paper round and for the winter of 1944/45 sold my wood.

We had bed bugs. My Dad said, 'Look here Harry Boy, loads of bed bugs.' This was the first time I had seen the bugs, they were just a bit smaller than a 5 pence piece. They hid away in and around your mattress and when you were fast asleep they bit you and sucked your blood, you would wake in the morning with bites all over your body. How did we get rid of them from the house? Mum called in the Council Inspectors and was told that due to the amount of bugs we would have to evacuate the house for at least 3 days. The council set the date for us to be out and they came in with sulphur candles to remove them. I stopped at Albert Brown's house 3 doors down the road and Mum and Dad found another place to stay. On our return you could still smell the sulphur around the house for days.

1945 and the war was still going on in Europe, with the troops of all nations doing well against the Germans, pushing and pushing them back. Then Hitler introduced his new weapon, the V2 Rocket. You could not hear it, could not see it, but if you were unlucky you would feel it. One Saturday afternoon in New Cross, South East London, the Woolworth's store was packed with Mums, Dads and kids, when one of these monster rockets made a direct hit on the store. There was much fatality and badly wounded families; the casualty list was very high. These V2s were dropping all over and Sir Winston Churchill ordered the V2 sites to be destroyed.

I left school and started work as a porter at Honor Oak Park railway station, near Forest Hill. My job was to sweep up, clean the toilets, close the train doors and do as I was told. My hours were from 6 am to 2 pm one week and 2 pm to 10 pm the following week.

One day, as I swept the platform a steam engine stopped right near me and a young man called out, 'Hi kid, how are you going?'

'OK,' I replied.

'How much do you get a week?'

I stuck out my chest and said, 'One pound 13 shillings and 8 pence a week.'

The young lad laughed and said, 'I get 19 quid a week.'

At that moment I could not swallow, I seemed to be struck dumb. I had never seen £19.

The lad said, 'Get down to the Bricklayers Arms,' (the railway depot) 'to the steam engine, and get on the footplate as a stoker.'

I asked my foreman George, who said that if I were to put in for a transfer it could take months, the best way would be to leave after giving notice. So I did just that.

On my arrival at the Bricklayers Arms, I asked if I could see the manager and within minutes I was in his office. I told this gentleman my story and handed him a letter that George had given me for this purpose. He said, 'Your old boss has written that you are a hard worker, that is good, it's what we need here.' I was told I would be engine cleaning until I was 16 years old, then would be in the shunt yard until a service route came up. The cleaning money would be good, with regular hours 7 am to 3 pm, with half an hour stop for tea and eats, and be supplied with the cloths for cleaning the engines.

*****

Engine cleaning was dirty work but the pay compensated for this. We had fun with the Cleaning Foreman. We would hide up in the roof and coo like the pigeons, and Tommy Tucker would shout, 'I know you little b***s are up there.' However, despite this he was a nice guy to us cleaners and was potty about 'safety first'. When we were cleaning an engine we had so many safety boards around the engine that it would cause a problem in cleaning, but he was right, no one I heard of was ever hurt within the engine cleaning department.

When I turned 16 I was able to work in the truck yard, which they called the shunt yard. You would go backwards and forwards more times than a clock pendulum. It was a bore but to get a service route you had to do this.

One day in 1947 Mum woke me at 3.30 am and said, 'Harry Boy, it's snowing and it's deep, you cannot go to work today,' this was because I cycled to work. I told her I would walk and I did, all the way to the Old Kent Road. I thought that if Chaucer made that long walk to Canterbury, I could walk to work, it was only about 6 miles. As I walked I thought of the films showing at the 2 Picture Houses opposite the railway yard in the Old Kent Road.

I arrived at work at about 5.15 am to have the foreman say to me, 'Where have you come from?'

I replied, 'Not from a hot country,' and then went on to say, 'Please can I dry my socks as my feet are wet?'

'OK, get dry and report to the manager at 10 am.'

'What for?'

'It's good news. If you can walk to work from Dulwich in this weather we need good timekeepers.'

At 10 am I was at the managers door, knocked on the door and heard, 'Come in.'

'You wanted to see me, sir?'

'Yes, Harry, can you finish at 12 noon today, go home, get some sleep and then return back here for 10 pm to meet your new driver Mr Harry Ball. Harry does the Hastings paper train run, it has passenger and morning papers on it.'

At this stage I was ready to walk out the door shouting, 'Great, great!' However, I said, 'Yes sir, I will be here tonight.'

I returned home at 12 noon to tell Mum and Dad my good news.

At 10 pm I was back looking for Harry Ball the train driver and it did not take long for me to decide that I liked him. He said, 'Come Harry Boy, let's walk to London Bridge Station.' I said, 'Walk when we have steam engines?' 'It's only round the corner.' We started to walk and he asked questions about my family and would I like to become a train driver, just general chat, whilst on the way to London Bridge Station. We arrived 15 minutes later as Harry knew the short cut to the station. Our engine was the L class, 2 passenger carriages and 3 trucks for the papers. We pulled out at about 11.30 pm. I worked on this job for another 7 months.

1948 - 1953
ARMY LIFE

After leaving the railway I did this job and that job; I was like a fish out of water. I saw this girlfriend and that girlfriend, the best one being Carol, we did get on well together. Indoors, Mum and Dad were still fighting, same old thing every weekend, so in the middle of 1948 I signed up for 5 years in the army, the Royal Tank Regiment. I was told I would have to wait until I was 17 and a half to go in, so having passed the medical, waited for my orders and went in around Christmas time.

Before I enter the army, let's look back at my early years. My sisters and I saw the black side of life. As you grow older you register more things in your brain, like who really started the fighting, Mum or Dad? Every weekend this would go on. When the school would break up for half term my sister Kath and I could not go out because Mum would pawn our clothes for drinks, so we just stood in our vests as we did not have underpants. My sister Kath and I stood by our bay window

13

and looked at the other kids playing and we cried, and then had bread and jam for lunch.

Why is beer more important than children are?

This went on for a long time, until a lady moved in next door. My sister Ellen said that this lady was a moneylender, but this was only talk, or was it? Because when we had another school holiday mum did not pawn our clothes. Or was that the time that I shouted and screamed at them, got a pair of scissors and slashed the settee in temper? My sister Kath and I had had enough, the pub was Mum and Dad's life, we, the kids just made up the numbers. But we did love them.

Ellen was now married with a baby son, Kath had joined the land army girls, and I was going into the army, otherwise I could have ended up on the wrong side of the street. My sister Ellen took me to Kings Cross Station on Sunday night, 6 January 1949 for the 6 pm train to Barnard Castle in Yorkshire.

My last words before I left home were, 'I love you Mum and Dad,' and I meant it.

The train ride from London to Barnard Castle was about 6 hours. Whilst we were on the move I thought to myself, 'What am I doing with my life? Here I am riding into the unknown; I have no idea what tomorrow will bring. My family, Ellen with her baby son Alan, Kath who is in the land army, well, Mum and Dad it's the pub life, I just hope I can make a life from this.'

On our arrival at the camp, we all lined up to collect our blankets, knife and fork, and billycan, then were taken to the barracks to unload our gear. It was the early hours of Monday morning now, so it was time to get under the blanket fast and sleep.

0600 hours. The wake up call was at this time, then be at breakfast for 0630 hours. One hour later barrack cleaning and inspection. 0800 hours on parade. Whilst on parade I had a good look around, this intake must have been at least 250 blokes. As green as green we marched off to get our hair cut. Some started marching with the left foot but many started with the right, what a laugh. The Corporals and the Sergeants were shouting like mad at us, words I just cannot use. These Corporals and Sergeants had 3 weeks to do our square bashing – meaning to learn to march up and down, keep in step with each other and as one makes a move you all look as one.

I had been at this camp for one month and the square bashing had gone well, so we got a 48 hour pass, Friday evening to Monday morning at 0800 hours. I had been given my pass and return railway ticket to Kings Cross. I arrived home at 11.30 pm that Friday night, put my hand into the letterbox for the key which is always on the string behind the door, but tonight no key.

I called through the letterbox, 'Mum, Dad, its Harry Boy, let me in please, the key is missing on the door.'

Mum shouted back, 'Go away, you are a deserter. The police and Red Caps have been here looking for you.'

I said, 'Do leave off, I have a pass,' and then I said, 'Dad, you know a pass when you see one.'

Dad looked at the pass and said, 'Let him in, it's a good pass.'

The next morning Dad and I went to the police station at Crystal Palace Road, East Dulwich.

'Please sort out this mess, officer, I am on leave but I have been posted as a deserter, and if that's the case why do I have an Army rail warrant?'

We waited for an answer from the Army; it took about an hour to do. Then 'It's all clear son, enjoy the rest of your time.'

On my return back I did a bit of shouting myself, about the mess someone had made.

That camp was not that bad. Regimental Sergeant Major May – no not the month, that was his name – shouted and balled about, but it was for the best, 'Do it now, not later'. After all the training we were ready to move off to other places.

I went to Bovington, Dorset, and the Tank depot.

On parade one morning an officer said to me, 'How old are you son?'

I said, 'I will be 18 in May, Sir.'

'Sorry,' he said, 'you are too young to go overseas now, but you soon will go.'

On or around 1 August 1949, I was due to leave England, so I had one weeks leave, and I made the most of it. A trooper at Bovy (short for Bovington) had said I would be away for 3 years, so I did all the best things and even broke my own rules by having a pint with my Dad. As I gave Dad a big hug he said, 'I will not be here when you return.'

I said, 'Shut up, you and all will be here,' gave him another hug and stepped onto the tram.

As the tram pulled away I was looking at him all the time, with tears in my eyes. My Dad might like a pint but he had never hit or punched me, my Mum did that, and yet many a time I had deserved it.

The ship left Southampton for Libya.

Just before we got to the Bay of Biscay a sailor said to me, 'Eat lots of bread, mate, and only sip water in small amounts, the Bay is very rough.'

I did this as we entered the Bay and within minutes we saw waves of 30 feet high hitting the ship. Many troopers were very sick. The ship was going up and down, from side to side; you could not go to the loo as they were full with the sick troops.

We arrived at Tobruk. It was full of damaged ships from the Second World War, stern, bow and ships on their sides, what a mess. Tobruk itself was in ruins, and danger signs were all over the place regarding booby traps. A brief history of this area. It was taken by the Italians, but in 1941 we the Brits took it, then the Germans from us, but we did not want that to happen did we, so in 1942 we took it back again.

We made our way to the town of Barce, about 2 to 3 hours ride away and *was* it hot in the back of the truck? We were met by the duty officer who welcomed us to the 13/18 Hussars. The next day I was made camp policeman just for 1 day. I watched prisoners digging a trench and when we got to the NAAFI I bought them a shandy each.

However, a sergeant caught us and I was marched off to the duty officer and told 'We don't do things like that here.'

'Sir, it must be hot in the shade, I would not put a dog out in that heat.'

'Trooper Benton, you can help them for the rest of the day.'

So there I was digging a hole; I made the prisoners laugh by saying that I wondered if I could make a square hole. It did me no harm to do a bit of digging.

A few days later I had my fortune told. This Arab said that many British officers came back to be told more, so he told my fortune.

'You will leave here soon and go away.'

I dived in and said, 'Home?'

'No,' he said, 'the other way, you will have a death in the family.'

'That's my Dad.'

'You will marry twice, have 2 sons, and you will win lots of money,' and then he had a face of horror.

I said, 'What is wrong?'

He did not answer me, just said 'It's nothing.'

Early in 1950 we moved the regiment to Egypt, a place called Ismaliya, a transit camp. We stayed here until the middle of May 1950 when we left to go to Malaya, crossing the Indian Ocean. Whilst on ship the troops were informed by way of lectures about Communism. I went along and found them useful. We arrived in Singapore and travelled through Johore to Kluang. Here we put up tents and cut back the jungle. I was not looking and a nest of red ants, about 1 inch long, dropped on me from a tree above. The other men rushed to my aid, brushing these ants off me. I was bitten very much and lumps appeared on my face, neck and arms.

Then there was the accident. The truck was a right off and I was left with a smashed ankle, even today I still have to visit an Orthopaedic Doctor plus appointments at the Medway

Hospital for the Disabled. Yes, over 50 years later I am still in pain with my left ankle, but I cannot blame the regiment. Being stuck in a remote place where could you find an Orthopaedic Doctor to repair the broken bones. The camp doctors said, 'You are excused wearing boots,' but the boots were the main support for my ankle. My boxing days were over.

A friend of mine, Sammy said to me that he had found out that the 3rd Tanks were in Hong Kong and should we go there? I said, 'yes' and within 6 weeks of putting our names down for transfer Sammy and I were on our way. Arriving in Hong Kong we soon settled down in 'B' Squadron and met some very good mates, Ken Lockabie, Sid Ardblaster and Jock Campbell, and we lived in brick built buildings, not tents.

I made a visit to the gym where I met a guy called Ken Holwood, boxing under the name of Ken Regan. In 1954 he was a contender for the light welterweight of the UK, boxing at the Winter Gardens, Blackpool. Ken wanted me to box with him but I had to tell him, 'Ken, I cannot do 3 rounds without pain, so how do you expect me to do 6 or 10 rounds?' This entire problem came about from a truck accident in Malaya.

What can I say? I'd been on patrol around a small village near Kluang, about 100 miles from Singapore, somewhere around 10 pm. Our camp was about 2 to 3 miles up a road with hairpin bends. There was some talking and shouting going on above the noise of the engine, and then it happened. One minute on the road, the next we were heading for a monsoon ditch. Have you even seen one of those ditches? The one that we hit was 6 feet across and 6 feet deep. We took off from the road and over the side down into this ditch. All I will say is that I was not the only one left with broken bones. That is the cause of the problem with which I still suffer today.

We had an Irish guy with us, Our Paddy. I asked him to stop the Chinese from using our toilet by putting up a sign. 'OK,' he said. Two days later there was a sign saying, 'Out of bounds to all Chinese.'

I walked into our building and said, 'Well done Paddy, good sign.'

'You like it?' he said.

'Yes,' I replied, 'but only one thing wrong. How do you expect a rice field Chinese man to read English, can you read Chinese?'

Paddy then had to get someone to translate the sign into Chinese for him.

On one occasion I collected all my smalls to be washed, putting them on my bunk. There was some shouting from outside, so I stepped out to see what was going on, but it was just a couple of troopers messing around. So off I went to wash my smalls and hang them up to dry. On returning to my bunk there were some more smalls left there. I called out for who had left them there, and then the giggling started.

'Come on,' I shouted, 'move this lot or I'll throw them outside.'

Sid said, 'Harry mate, these are your smalls.'

'I have just washed mine.'

'Sorry, but you have just washed mine, these are yours, I swapped them over when you went outside earlier.'

This had the whole barrack in laughter.

I was sent back to Malaya in the North Kedah.

Whilst in the Kedah area I was asked to pick up an officer from near Penang. I had an escort for the 'red road' and we had no problems. After saying goodbye to the escort I passed through a little village, kids running all over the road and around the straw houses, so now I watched for anyone running towards the Land Rover. My speed was only about 12 miles an hour and then it happened. *Bang!* on the vehicle. I stopped dead, jumped out, rushed to the front of the Land Rover and there was a small boy about 10 years old lying near the front nearside wheel. He was out cold. Within seconds the crowd had grown. I said, 'Mum, where is Mum?' An Indian woman was looking at me; I touched her and said,

'Mum?' The lady nodded and then said, 'First aid, Red Cross,' and pointed to a straw hut about 800 yards up the road.

I grabbed the lady's arm, put her in the front seat, picked up the lad and placed him on his mother's lap, then drove to the hut. I carried the lad in and laid him on the bed. Thank God the doctor spoke good English. I told him the story while the boy's mother prayed. I asked the doctor what she was doing and he replied, 'The lady thinks you are very kind to the lad and she is praying for you.' Before I left the doctor told me not to worry about the boy, as he would soon be as good as new. Three weeks later I was called into the Officer's office and he told me, 'I have just had a letter from a doctor, and he said how good you were with a little boy and his mother. This will be put on your records.'

We had good weekend breaks in Penang Island. In our camp we had the Dayak or Dyak, these were headhunters from Borneo, and the Johnny Gurkhas. With all these men around you could sleep peacefully. After our weekend in Penang Island we would make our way back to our camp at Hong Kong know as Sek Kong, which was about 20 miles up country. The lads preferred me to drive the truck, as I did not drink, only shandy. On returning to our camp safely I knew that I had put their minds at rest that the truck would not go off the side of the mountain.

Early in 1952 our King passed away; we had a big parade for him. Then I lost my Dad. I cried, as I was only weeks away from seeing him again and being able to buy him a pint in the Cherry Tree.

Around 22 February the regiment left Hong Kong for home, stopping at Singapore. Then across the Indian Ocean to Kenya, up to Aden, then the Red Sea and to the Suez Canal. The length of the Canal is 99 miles; therefore there are bays for ships to pass by each other. We stopped at Bitter Lakes near Ismailiya, where we were in the 13/18 Hussars. This took me back to the night of the shooting.

A group of us had been swimming in or near Bitter Lakes and arrived back at camp in time for our tea. After tea we just sat playing a game of cards or talking. Then we heard shooting, so rushed out of the tent and headed for where the sound had come from. The man doing the shooting was Polish (we had a large amount of Polish men and women in our forces). Corporal Edwards said to get his attention. We all started to talk to the trooper, things like, 'What's up mate?' 'Are you alright?' and in the meantime Corporal Edwards crept around to the back of him. He jumped on his back whilst we wrestled the gun from his hand. The Polish trooper was taken to the Guard Room and then taken away by the Egyptian police. This man had killed 2 and wounded 2 in the Dobie Wallar tent. What is a Dobie Wallar? They were people who cleaned our khaki, which is the dull yellowish brown colour of our military uniform. Dobie Wallar is in fact Arabic for Iron Shop. These people worked on your uniform, cleaned and ironed it. So the name is Iron Shop in English and Dobie Wallar in Arabic.

And the story goes like this.

That night, the Polish trooper had wanted to become stick-man. What is a stick-man? A stick-man is the title given to the smartest man on guard duty and entitled him to be dismissed from his duty. The story we were told was that the Polish trooper asked the Dobie Wallars to give extra care to his khaki, as he wanted that title that particular night. Talk was that he had met a local girl and was due to see her that night, the night of his guard duty. However, he had been put on duty as somebody else had gone 'tom and dick', that's sick. So as to keep his date with this girl he had called in to see the local workers in the Dobie Wallar tent, and then when he had not been awarded the title of stick-man, that night he just went bananas.

We moved from Bitter Lakes to Port Said (pronounced Side) at the end of the Suez Canal as it joins the Mediterranean Sea. We were looking over the side of the ship where there were floating barrow boys in their canoes who would shout up,

'Hello Johnny, you want top good tea set for your lovely lady when you get home?' We asked how much and got the reply, 'Only 2 pounds Johnny.' I was only earning £2 a week, however another crewmember said, 'OK, send up your basket.' The Egyptian barrow boy had a rope with a heavy lead weight at one end, which he would swing round and round, then sling the lead weight up on to the deck. You then pulled on the rope and up came the basket. Inside the basket was a peg next to a little hook, on to which was clipped the £2 and then lowered over the side down to the canoe, and the tea set then came back up. The crewman took his tea set away but within minutes he was dashing back on to the deck shouting to the lad, 'Hey, you f*** Egyptian, that tea set is broken.' We heard shouting back up to the deck and the crewman asked us to keep the lad talking while he dashed off. The lad asked where he had gone and we replied, 'To show you the broken bit of the tea set.' I then looked around to see the crewman with a 56lbs sack of potatoes on his back, which he then dropped on to the deck. He called for the barrow boy to come close to the ship so that he could see the damage to the tea set. The barrow boy moved in like a rat in a trap, the crewman picked up the sack of spuds and dropped the 56lbs on to the front of his canoe. The goods and the boy were shot into the air and landed in the water. That, I will always remember!

The Bay of Biscay was calm like a millpond. We did not then go to Southampton but to Liverpool Docks, where I was given my rail ticket and sent off on 3 months Python leave (that being a long leave).

When I arrived home, Mum looked pale, thin and aged. However, with a big smile I said, 'Hi Mum, you do look great.' We sat and talked about Dad, to die at the age of 52 years old was not much of a life.

I went to the Cherry Tree with Mum so that all her friends could see me, but only stopped for about 30 minutes. I wanted to look for my old pals so walked up Lordship Lane looking in the pubs, but was unable to find any.

My sister Ellen arranged a party for my 21st birthday at her house. The house was not big, but it was a good party and lots of fun, a few army blokes turned up along with my old pals from Dulwich, and just 1 or 2 girls.

The following Saturday I met the most beautiful person in the world, Betty Elson, just fab! We all said that we would meet that night and bus it to the pub the Hornes in Clapham Road. We were in the Hornes for 2 or 3 hours then went back to Dulwich. The bus always stopped on top of Doggy where there was a dance being held in my old school, so we jumped off the bus and paid to go into the dance. Things were going well until a problem came up, and I'm sorry to say a fight broke out. There was shouting and crying, but I said, 'Come on, we don' need this,' and we all went our separate ways.

I took Betty home, who lived in Ledbury House, Pitchley Road off Doggy. Betty's mum and dad came home and we had a long chat about the army overseas. Betty's dad was in Italy during the Second World War. From the start of meeting them we got on well together, we sat and talked until about 2 am.

So now I could call on Betty with their consent, and I met Betty at work, she worked at the Law Courts, which is the Royal Court of Justice in Fleet Street. This building was built by an architect called Street at the cost of £800,000 in style of Monastic Gothic. From there we 'bused' it home. Going over Blackfriars Bridge we saw an advertising board with Tony Bennett and I told Betty that we had heard him singing from Radio Milan in Hong Kong before he was known in the UK.

I met Betty more and more before my python leave was up. The regiment was down in Warminster and my return I got a real blast from the CO for late return back.. The regiment was on the move again, to a German town called Detmold. On 9 September 1952 we were off, taking 2 days to get to Germany, overnight ferry and then a long train ride.

We had inter-Squadron boxing and I was in charge of 'B' Squadron, so I went around the chaps getting them to back up their Squadron. The best fight one particular night was Jock Campbell and David Fry. What a fight! Jock could just stare at you and the stare would frighten you to death, and David could run very fast, in those days he was particularly good at the 440 yards. The first round started and Jock went like a cannon ball after David. But David, with those fast legs, moved well and at the same time punching Jock. At the end of the first round I told Jock to get David in the corners and sling punches at him. The second round was ours, but David Fry did not let that happen again, he moved from left to right. Poor old Jock could not hold him down. It was good.

I was soon called to the CO's office and told I was being posted to Ash near Aldershot, so I said goodbye to one and all. Sid Ardblaster and I had had fun, but I had to go, again the journey time from Germany back to England being 2 days.

Mons Camp was for officer cadets; Mons is named after a place in Europe where bad fighting took place during the First World War.

I drove different vehicles whilst there and got on well with the cadets. The best was to drive up to the Hogs Back, where we would have a shandy and food, but these chaps were there to lean and that's what they did.

Our Regimental Sergeant Major was a man called Tibby from the Welsh Guards, and he was big. He would pedal his old bike and shout at the top of his voice, 'You there, stand still.' Then he would ride up to you, walk round you and say, 'Am I hurting you lad?'

You would reply in a quiet voice, 'No sir.'

He would then shout at the top of his voice, 'I should be, I am standing on your hair,' and then walk away saying, 'I have never seen anything like it in all my life.'

Does anybody remember this great guy?

One day by accident I had to go to the guardroom where I saw Tibby and another officer, and I'm afraid I was ear wigging their conversation.

Tibby was saying, 'Where can we find another dispatch rider for tonight?'

I turned and said, 'Sir, do you have a need for a dispatch rider?'

'Yes, we need one urgently to go to Sandhurst.'

I said, 'I will do it.'

'Have you a licence?' Out comes my licence. Then, 'Do you know the way?'

'Yes sir,' and I was gone.

I missed my dinner but this good deed helped me a lot. I did a lot more motor bike riding for the camp and of course had more freedom this way.

I was demobbed in November 1953 and I would say to any young man, *If your life is upside down and you don't know what to do, join the army. Put up with the shouting, it's a great life, and it will make a man out of you.*

DEMOBBED

During 1954 I started driving for Hall & Co Ltd in East Dulwich. The vehicle was a 5-yard tipper – 5 yards being like 5 tons – and we carried sand and ballast from the pits to the building sites. We made about 4 or 5 runs a day and were paid £5 or £6 a week, plus £1 each month for a clean truck. The hours were 6 am to 6 pm with lunch at any time.

One day I had 5 yards of sand for the building site at the top of Lordship Lane. Today there is a block of flats there, just before the Grove Tavern, which is now a Harvester. Well, going back to 1954, I shouted to the blokes, 'Where do you want me to tip?'

One chap shouted back, 'Over here.'

'Is the ground safe?'

'Yes,' was the reply.

So I started to back up with the sand and the next thing I knew I was looking at the sky and the thumb on my right hand was giving me a lot of pain. I climbed out of the cab and looked at my tipper, which looked like a rocket ready for take-off.

The builders said, 'How did you do that?'

'Simple,' I replied, 'I listened to you guys saying back over here, come back, come back and then this.'

Our depot was only a mile away so the manager came along and blamed me for the accident

I said, 'Oh yes, I see what you mean, I came here and dug this great hole and then backed the truck into it.'

My tipping days were over, but I still managed to have use of the truck to get to Fleet Street on Fridays.

Betty Elson and I got engaged. Betty still worked in the Law Courts and one day saw a second-hand ring going for £25 at a jeweller in Fleet Street. One Saturday we went to the jewellers, the ring was still there, so I laid down £2 deposit and paid off the balance over 10 weeks, using the old tipper truck to get me there each Friday.

I now wanted to get my coach licence and in order to do this I met up with a bloke called Lenny Pailthorpe; he looked like Ronald Reagan the actor. We hired a coach from Horseferry coaches and made our way to the Lambeth Bridge (PSV) Office. An officer came out and we were on our way. We drove around Hyde Park Corner, Piccadilly, Oxford Street and back home to Lambeth, the man got out and said, 'You have both passed. Benton, you must see the Head of Traffic Officer.' I went to his office and was asked if I was still in contact with 5 or 6 people that he then named. I told him, ' If I should see these gentlemen and the pub was open I would have a shandy with them, but if I was asked to do something which I don't like I would not be rude to them or about it, but I would reject their offer.' The officer then handed me my Public Service Vehicle Licence or PSV, although today it is no longer known as that.

One day I was travelling along the Crystal Palace Road, East Dulwich, and I noticed that the top flat of number 325 was empty. I knocked on the door and an old man answered.

'Hi,' I said, 'is the top flat going empty?'

'Yes.'

'How much is the rent a week?'

'£3.'

'OK,' I said, 'here is £3 now, just give me a receipt and we will be back tonight.'

Betty liked it and so we booked our wedding for 13 November 1954 at the Town Hall in Peckham.

I had now worked out what to do with my life, drive coaches in the summer and do coaling in the winter; it kept the cash rolling in. Coaling would be to shovel coals into sacks, load them onto a truck and then travelling the roads and selling them, or 'trolleying' them

I met up with Big Fred Worthington, who stood 6 foot 4 inches. Big Fred's mum and dad were the kindest people you could ever come across; in fact the whole family was great. I worked with Fred on coaling all over the EastEnd and SouthEast of London. We made a living, that's all, but I was a bloody fool and was now into gambling. And then when the summer came I worked for Charlie Banfields at Banfield Coaches.

My son Tony was born on 13 January 1957, weighing just over 7lbs, and he had the same eyes as me. However, Betty and Tony could not leave the hospital straight away because of Tony's eyes which were crusted up, and they remained there for about 3 weeks until they had cleared up.

I passed Hall & Co depot on route to and from the hospital and one day bumped into the manager, who asked me how I was.

I said, 'I am sorry that you stopped and asked me that. One, I am far better off. Two, when I had that tip up with your vehicle, I broke the thumb on my right hand. Remember I said my thumb hurt, well, it was painful for 2 or 3 weeks after that. I went to Dulwich Hospital for a x-ray and was told I had a broken thumb. Now I will say this to you. I was not in the wrong, but it did me good, as I now know not to put any trust in p*** like you. The men working on that site knew the site like the back of their hands, so now if anyone says it is OK, I always check it out.' And I then walked away from him.

We had a lot of problems with Jimmy Crook who also lived in the flats. Bits of food peelings were being dropped down the toilet and kept blocking it up. Betty then had to use the toilet in the bottom flat, which was rented by another couple with twins. I called at the Estate Agent but he just turned a deaf ear, so I went to the Town Hall and saw the Environmental Officer. He said, 'Go back to the Estate Agent, tell them you have seen me and that I want a new toilet put in by 3 pm today. If they give you any problem, ring me.' I did just that, nothing happened, so I phoned the Environmental Office and by 2.30 pm there was a new toilet being put in.

Still Jimmy Crook continued throwing things down the toilet and blocking it up again, and by now we had had it up to our necks with him.

We moved back in with Mum and I said to Betty, 'We cannot stay here too long. You will see a good side of Mum during the day and then a bad side at night, like Jekyll and Hyde.' At night the drink turned Mum into a different person. We did not see this for about 6 weeks and then it came out, my Mum of old, yet we could not avoid her and just got used to this way of life.

It was summer time of 1958 and Banfield Coaches were full to the brim on all runs. At night I would go the Dogs at Catford, but I could not win, my luck was right out.

These are true words for gambling, alcohol or sex; '*We are all controlled by our passions, and we regret stupid things we have done for the rest of our lives, by destroying our loved ones and our families.*' How true.

On 4 September 1958 the start of the day was like any other day. I left home at 7.30 am, it was dry so I walked to Banfield Garage near Peckham Rye which takes about 10 minutes. I passed the Cherry Tree pub, along Grove Vale up to Goose Green, which is a small opening with a few trees and a tuft of grass here and there. Over the years it has given

28

my friends and I a lot of fun, as kids we would come out of Dulwich Swimming Baths and kick a ball around Goose Green. Passing the council kiddies swings and slide reminds me of my old days, a snotty nosed kid with holes in my socks and trousers. Boy, does this bring back memories. Today, yes, I do have a hole in my sock, but that is my nutty way of living, by gambling my wages and tips away.

On arriving at the garage I always called out, 'I'm in,' and a fitter would reply, 'OK Harry.' The coach I had been driving was a Leyland, Burlington body with 39 seats. Unloaded its weight was 10 tons but with a full passenger load, with a mixture of mums, dads and kids, up to about 20 tons. This particular day my work sheet read Southend-on-Sea, the pick-up points and names of those to pick up, and the last pick up point was at Mr Banfield's sister, Nicky's, kiosk.

Nicky's kiosk was in Walworth Road, SouthEast London opposite Liverpool Grove – do you remember Walworth, the one who slew Wat Tyler? My route took me to the Elephant and Castle, across Tower Bridge and out towards the East, Southend is only 40 miles away so the passengers had a nice steady ride. Stopping at the Bull pub on the way I shouted, '15 minutes only.' You always got someone asking why we had stopped, I would speak softly and explain that some may have waterworks problems, so whether the trip was short or long I would always stop.

Travelling towards Southend we went through Leigh-on-Sea, and this was the start of a bad day. My speed was 20 to 25 mph, past shops and streetlights, it was a built-up area, and then it happened!

I saw a woman walking straight into the path of the coach. I pulled the coach to the right, braking at the same time. There was a bollard in the centre of the road that I just missed and managed to stop very quickly. Whilst doing this I heard a thud, this being the woman striking the coach. The passengers were shouting and crying, however I left the coach where it had stopped and got out to see the woman lying on the pavement. I rushed to the nearest shop shouting, 'Phone

29

for an ambulance!' As I arrived back at the scene of the accident a kind lady offered me a cup of tea; she only lived close by in a corner house on the side street. I asked the passengers to inform the police of my whereabouts and followed this lady to her house. Within minutes the police were knocking at the door wanting to see me.

'It's alright son,' said the officer, 'let's see your running sheet.' A running sheet is a Ministry of Transport route sheet. It stated that Banfield had been given the service route into Southend along the A13; it also stated the number of passengers to ensure the coach was not overloaded.

I stood with the police for 40 minutes answering questions about the vehicle, whilst they kicked the tyres to check for air. I told them that Banfield had the Ministry of Transport Engineers in the garage often twice a week, had the best equipment in south London, pits, cranes, power units, and that the coach had vacuum brakes. Whilst I was talking to the police the injured lady was taken to Southend General Hospital. I did not have the coach insurance or my driving licence on me and was given 5 days to produce them at East Dulwich nick (police station).

I was then able to continue driving the passengers into Southend but felt upset and bad all day long. I telephoned Banfield and told him what had happened.

'What time do you think you will get home?' I was asked.

I told him, 'The passengers are shaken up and I feel sick about the whole thing.'

'OK, we will see you tonight on your return.'

I left Southend around 5.30 pm and must have said sorry to the passengers about 100 times. However, they knew that my speed had been all right and that I was steady.

On my arrival at Banfield garage at 7.45 pm, the only person around was Omo, our engineer.

He said, 'Sorry to hear about the problem Harry.'

I asked, 'Where are all the tops to see me?'

'Gone home and will see you tomorrow morning.'

I looked at the next day's work sheet and saw that I was down for another job.

'That's out Omo,' I shouted, 'I must go to the police station and will not be in until 10 o'clock. Let them know.'

On arriving home just after 8 pm, Betty the wife was watching the TV and my son Tony was fast asleep. I told Betty the whole of the day's story, she gave me a great deal of comfort and then I took 2 Aspro tablets to help me sleep. During the night I tossed and turned, daylight came, and I got up to make the tea and toast for us all. When Tony got up, boy did I give him one big hug; he was about 18 months old by now.

I made my way to work and Mr Banfield was standing at the garage doors.

'Morning Harry,' he said. I replied the same.

'What is your work today son?' he said.

'Mr Banfield, I need the Company Insurance Certificate for coach KAB 555.'

He told me the certificate covered all the vehicles, so I said that I would not be long, but must take it to the police station. On arriving at the station I told the story to the guy booking in the information, to which he said, 'Let's hope the lady is all right.'

On returning to the garage, Mr Banfield said, 'I've put you on a small job this afternoon.'

'Sorry Mr Banfield,' I replied, 'but I want to be with my family today, so I will see you tomorrow.' And with that I left the garage.

The next day I was on a service run to Margate, Broadstairs and Ramsgate. If he had given me a pub outing I could not have taken the job; I just wanted to have a quiet day. I did the run, dropped off the passengers at the coast and picked up those returning to London. On this particular run the driver is always home for tea, so I was walking in at home at about 4.30 pm, nice and early. That night we just sat and watched the TV and then I had another early night.

Sunday morning, 7 September 1958, I had just shaved and washed the soap from my face when there was a knock at the front door. I opened the door with the towel still in my hand, to a policeman.

'Good morning sir,' he said, 'are you Mr Henry Thomas Benton.'

'Yes,' I answered.

'Sir, regarding the accident of Thursday last, the 4 September 1958, I am here to inform you that the lady who was taken to the hospital died this morning at 4.30. I am very sorry to tell you this, Mr Benton, but you must attend the Coroner's Inquest on Friday next, the 12 September 1958 at 11 am at Southend-on-Sea.

I awoke Betty and told her, then went to work and told Mr Banfield. He said, 'Drive the service coach.'

'Up your pipe,' I replied, 'I will travel down *on* the service coach, not driving it.' And that's what I did.

The following Friday I walked into Banfield garage at about 7.30 am. Mr Banfield called out, 'Harry, I have information for you. When you get to the inquest today, you will meet up with my solicitor, he is there to ensure that no-one tries to twist things around.' 'Thanks,' I said.

On arriving at the inquest I did meet the solicitor and said to him, 'Who are all these people?'

He replied, 'Don't worry, some are witnesses and others are local reporters.'

'Mrs Frances Bridgland, aged 75, widow of Canterbury, had been staying with her sister Mrs Read. Mrs Bridgland had just posted a letter and from the post box walked towards the centre of the London Road, this was the middle crossing on the A13 Main London Road, however she walked into the side of the coach. Mrs Bridgland was thrown back onto the kerb.'

P C Dipple said that he was standing by the bus stop when a grey coach approached in a stream of traffic, its speed was quite reasonable at between 25 and 30 mph. He saw an elderly woman crossing the road; she was thrown back onto the kerb. The coach pulled up in double its length and was over to the right as far as the bollard would allow.

I stated, 'I had left London at 9 am and we stopped at the Bull pub for a 15 minute break. When doing a short run like

Southend there is no need to rush, the time of the accident states that fact. I saw this woman walk towards the centre to the bollard, so I hooted, braked hard and swerved to my right whilst watching the bollard. I heard a thud which was the lady striking the side of the coach.

The Coroner said, 'There is no evidence of negligence by the driver, his speed and time shows that.' Mrs Read, the sister said that her sister had worn glasses and had a developing cataract in one eye. Dr D C Caldwell gave evidence that her death was due to multiple injuries including a fractured skull and considerable trauma.

The Coroner's verdict was that the woman walked into the road without looking what was coming along.

Sometime during 1959 Charlie Banfield said to me, 'Harry, I have a top job for you tomorrow. Pick up at 8.30 am at Vauxhall Bridge Road and Millbank, and take this party to Farnborough in Hampshire. It's a VIP job.

The next morning I was waiting on the corner, as there was not even room enough to park a bike along the road that day.

A chap came up and said, 'Are you the driver of this coach?'

'Yes sir.'

'Are you taking a party to Farnborough?'

'Yes sir.'

'That's good, I've got the right coach,' and when all the gentlemen had boarded I set off for Farnborough.

Once there I was asked to join them, to which I replied, 'Yes please.' I kept my distance from the group so as not to crowd them and we were taken to a lecture room where I sat at the back.

The lecture was about the De Havilland 106 Comet.

This plane was a complete breakaway from the piston engine and was the only sure way of wresting the wartime lead in aircraft transport from the Americans. A team led by R E Bishop, made several designs using goblin turbojets, a rear engine with Ghosts and a tailless type with swept wing and short fuselage. However when the new DH 106 was finalised it was on more orthodox lines.

The name Comet was revived and construction took place at Hatfield in considerable secrecy. On 27 July 1949 it flew for the first time at Hatfield, piloted by John Cunningham with a crew of 3.

Public demonstrations at Farnborough in September 1949 were followed by a number of fast overseas flights to measure fuel consumption under simulated airline conditions. This commenced with a return trip to Castel Benito, Libya, at an average speed of 448 mph, again piloted by John Cunningham on 25 October 1949.

On 2 May 1952 a regular day and a half scheduled service was introduced over the 10200 mile route between London and Tokyo. On 23 May 1952 Queen Elizabeth, the Queen Mother, Princess Margaret and Sir and Lady Geoffrey De Havilland made a Royal flight around Europe.

Then accidents began to occur.

On a Sunday night, 26 October 1952 at Ciampino, with a steady drizzle coming down, the Comet plane named Yoke Zebra taxied away in the glare of the apron lights, its wheels sending up little plumes of spray from the concrete. With 35 passengers on board it was bound for London.

A moment later a vicious judder told the captain that a stall was setting into the plane. Yoke Zebra fell heavily back onto the runway and the airport boundary was rushing up to meet them. The captain made a lightning decision to abandon the take-off, but as he reached out to close the throttles the aircraft hit a low mound of earth at the end of the runway and careered wildly on for a further 30 yards in a gigantic slither across the rough, rain softened ground. It came to rest only 10 yards short of the boundary fence. With the entire goings on the captain was congratulated for his skills.

More aircraft accidents happened, the Empress of Hawaii at Karachi in Pakistan on 2 March 1953, and on 2 May 1953 near Calcutta. On 15 January 1954, Yoke Peter cruising at 20000 feet in clouds that blanketed the Mediterranean, was less than an hour from take off in Rome, when the radio cut off.

'George, how Jig from George Yoke Peter, did you get me…..' and that was all.

Fishermen in the Mediterranean at around 11 am were hauling in their nets and peered up as the Comet's characteristic steady whine was interrupted by a series of shattering explosions that echoed thunderously back and forth across the grey sky. There was a long pause and a great shower of burning debris came hissing down out of the grey clouds and plunged into the sea. Bits of wreckage floated around but most of Yoke Peter lay beneath 400 feet of water.

Certificates of airworthiness were withdrawn.

Although we lost the air race for passenger jets, today our aircraft are the best.

I would like to say, this was one of the most interesting days of my life. They showed us a simulation of turbulence, by placing the fuselage of a plane inside a large tank of water, about 100 metres long. They then vibrated the tank to produce the impression of turbulence. To see the plane then split into 2, it did open my eyes!

INTO THE SIXTIES

During the early part of 1960 I started work at Wallis Bakery in Lewisham. The distance from Dulwich to Lewisham is about 6 or 7 miles through the back streets, but finding a bus at 4.15 am was not on, so I cycled as this was the only way to be at work on time.

My supervisor was a very smart chap, with good looks. My job was to sell bread on a route around Sidcup, Eltham, Bexleyheath, Crayford and Old Bexley, and this supervisor remained with me for my first 2 weeks. I would say he was a good salesman, but I was even better. The full takings for the week in those days were about £400, my wages were £6 or £7, then there was the fuel for the van which was filled up twice a week – the price of a gallon of petrol was 2/6d which

35

is half a crown, and there being 8 half crowns to a pound – so now you can see what kind of profit that made for the company.

Now I was ready to start selling by myself - remember the Bentons were costermongers. I was not to seem to be pushing the products but I needed to make the customers my good friends in order to succeed. I would sometimes ask them if I could add a loaf or 2 to their order if I had any over on my load, with an agreed sale or return. They would often agree to this, but not often did they need to return any as unsold, so I would return to the depot with an empty van and *up* went my sales.

At one time the weather had been bad, constant rain whilst doing my rounds, and I would have to just dry out whilst on the road. This went on for days, but my sales had now gone up to £450 a week and were still rising, and so I continued. Now I began to feel very sick and had a sore throat, and still the rain continued, raining 'cats and dogs' the whole time.

On returning to the depot I saw the manager and said, 'I will try to get into work tomorrow but I am not feeling too well.'

His reply was, 'You'd better come in.'

When I reached home I went straight to bed and when Betty came home with Tony she brought me a cup of tea. I told her I felt like I was dying and that I would go to the doctor at 5 pm.

My doctor was German, Doctor Handley, he was good, one of the best. However, he was not on duty that night, instead I saw my first lady doctor, Doctor Patel, who was also very good.

'Go home and collect this medicine on route,' she said, 'you have pleurisy of the lungs. Get into a warm bed and take a week off of work.'

I went home first and asked Betty to put some plates in the oven to warm up ready for my bed. Tony was sitting there and I said, 'Do you want to look after your Dad and walk with me to the chemist?' He jumped up, grabbed my hand and we both went to a little area in Dulwich known as the Ivanhoe – named after the local pub.

Whilst waiting for my medicine a big black man walked in. Tony said, 'Dad, that man has not washed his face.' Where could I look?

I just said to this big guy, 'Sorry mate, you are the first black man he has seen.'

He replied, 'No problem.'

I was too ill to explain anything to Tony.

At home, I fell into bed and went straight off to sleep. I kept waking up, drinking lots of water and at 2.30 am told Betty to phone for the doctor. The doctor was very quick, checked me over and said, 'Phone the hospital now, he has double pneumonia.' The ambulance was there in just 3 minutes and I was whipped into St Giles Hospital, Camberwell, this was where I had been born.

I had a tent over me and a tap inserted into my back to drain fluid. I did not seem to know where I was, whether on holiday or in a pub with that tap in my back. I was in there for 3 weeks and whilst there the manager from Wallis Bakers came to see me bringing with him my wage packets for 3 weeks. He told me that my job was safe, and I told him I would write, but I never did.

When I was better I went to see him and told him that he should start believing people. If I had tried coming to work on that day I could have died, leaving my wife and boy. Then I told him, 'You can take a running jump!'

Now I was back to working for Banfield Coaches again.

One evening I arrived home at about 8.30 pm. The nights were still light and very warm and sticky. Betty was watching the TV and Tony was fast asleep in our small bedroom. I noticed a fur coat on one of the chairs and asked, 'What is this doing here?' As I was saying this I noticed a large bag containing more fur coats with the price labels on for 2 or 3 grand.

'What the hell is going on around here? Have we opened a fur shop?'

The answer was that a friend of the family had been busy turning over a large store in SouthEast London and because he was well known with the Old Bill he thought he could leave the gear with us until things had cooled down. Betty continued saying that this person had left another bag in the bedroom. I crept in the bedroom so as not to awaken my small son, made my way to the cupboard, eased the door open, put my hand up to the top shelf and moved it around very slowly. I felt the bag and carefully removed it from the cupboard. The bag looked just like a doctor's brown leather bag and was about 10 to 12 inches long. I opened it and gasped. I was looking at a bag full of sweating (dangerous) dynamite!

My brain was telling me to think carefully and not to panic, but I was ready to blow my top. This 'dick head' had left this bag of destruction that could bring down the whole block of flats, which had just been rebuilt from the damage during the war. I looked at who could have been killed, my son Tony, wife Betty and all the rest of the people who would have been indoors at that time.

I moved very slowly into the front room, showed the contents of the bag to Betty and said, 'Did you know this is what that fool left in the bedroom cupboard?'

'No.'

I told her, 'I am taking this round to his house and will give him a few words about this dynamite.'

I made my way to my old banger and placed the dynamite on the front seat whilst I started up the car. The car started straight away, thank God, I then placed the bag on the floor because if I had to brake quickly the bag would shoot off the front seat and could explode. It would be a catastrophe if they were to find the car and myself all in bits and anybody nearby would cop it too.

I drove at a slow pace, about 15 mph around Goose Green and towards the Kings Arms pub at Peckham Rye. The traffic lights at the Kings Arms were green so I sailed through them and on to the 'nut's' house. Every pothole in the road I managed to drive through and it felt like the 2 miles was about 200 miles. On arriving at his house, the same movement on alighting from the car, very steady moves, I banged 3 times on his door and his wife opened it.

'Here love,' I said, 'take this very carefully, dig a hole in the middle of your garden, do it deep, then place this dynamite in it. Be very slow on moving the bag about as this dynamite is sweating. Then cover it with the dirt you have dug up, but do not pat the dirt down. When the nut comes home tell him to move the goods from my flat and do not come back.'

Do you know that those fur coats were worth more than some 2 or 3 bedroom houses in those early days of the sixties?

The nut? Well I did not see him again for years.

Banfield Coaches along with many other coach companies, was awarded the Council Schools contract. This meant they could pick up at a school anywhere within the SouthEast area of London and take them to Ewell, near Sutton in Surrey. At Ewell were the playing fields for the London concrete schools, those who only had hard stones and concrete to run about on, and to be able to enjoy sports like the posh kids somebody came up with a good idea. This was to take the kids out for 2 hours in the morning or afternoon to Ewell, we the drivers always got back to the garage at about 4.30 pm, and then at 5 pm our work for the next day was pinned up on the board.

It was 1961 and I had just done the 2 schools for that day and was waiting for the orders to go up for the next day's work. Mr Banfield came down and shouted, 'Patsie Weller and Harry Benton, you are on standby.' What does this mean? Banfield Coaches had the Isle of Grain contract; the Isle of Grain is in the Medway near Rochester in Kent. The contract was for 400 coaches or buses to ferry the workers to and from the building of the Power Station. This meant that Patsie and I were on standby until 9 pm when all the vehicles should have finished their runs. If any of them had any problems they would ring the garage and talk to the fitter and

39

we would be there if we were needed. So Patsie and I were stuck there for the night. I popped indoors to tell Betty and then Patsie went home to inform his wife.

That night the phone rang and it was the driver of a double-decker bus who had a flat tyre, and was parked in the car park just off the A2 near Canterbury Cathedral. At that time the M2 had not been built and the old A2 was used, so this meant that the route was through all the Medway towns. As we got to Dunkirk Hill I saw the red ignition light come on, meaning that the fan belt had broken and we were now right deep in it. We managed to get to the bus with the flat tyre, changed it and then rang the fitter at the garage and asked him to bring out battery, fan belt, fags and money. We eventually got home at 5.30 am, had a wash and shave and I was back to take the 2 schools again for that day.

So Patsie and I did a shift of 32 hours without any sleep. I think today you are only allowed to do 11 hours. What would the Ministry do today if we still did those kinds of hours, but remember it was not the fault of the coach operators, but that of the government of the day.

If you went on a Beano – that's an outing to the coast – you would stop on the way at a pub. The first thing you would hear was, 'Buy a pint for the driver.' And you would have to drink it!

We had no log book to record our hours, no tacograph disk, just a sheet of pick-up times, the pick-up points and then where to take the passengers, wait for them and then return. If your wife asked what time you would be in, what could you say? 'When I get home. It may be today or even tomorrow. Sorry love, see you when I see you.' What a way to live!

When I started back with Charlie Banfield I had asked him to keep me away from the Beano runs. So I was given the old folk to take to the coast and was back at about 7 pm, that was good. However, one Saturday I had a work sheet that read to pick up at the Imperial College, Exhibition Road, South Kensington, and take to Sheffield, wait and then return home. The pick-up time was for 11 am on that Saturday morning. After picking up about 20 young lads we were soon on our way to Sheffield.

On arriving there, I said, 'What part of Sheffield do you want?'

The answer I got was, 'No, we are going up to the hills and to the other side.'

'You are joking, yes?'

'No mate. We are potholers.'

Well, I drove up this hill and down, then around another until finally we reached the place at about 5 pm.

'What time do you want picking up tonight?'

'Not tonight mate, make it about 12 noon tomorrow.'

I was dumbfounded. I had about 4 shillings on me and was stuck in the middle of nowhere. I drove down to the city and parked in a shopper's car park, opened the doors and sat on the steps of the coach. Just then a copper walks up and tells me that I cannot park there.

I said, 'Give over mate, I've just taken a load of nutty potholers up in those hills. I did not know I was going to be here all night, just look at my running sheet.'

The copper did so and was now on my side. He told me there was a fish and chip shop just around the corner and that as long as I stayed with the coach I could park it there.

I then asked him, 'Where is the police station?'

'Why?' he said.

'To beg for a cup of tea in the morning,' I told him.

Soon I put my head down on the back seat of the coach and went to sleep.

The next morning I was back up in the hills waiting for the young men to return back to London. Leaving at about 1 pm we were back home by 7 pm, including some stops on the way.

As soon as I walked indoors I said, 'That's it, we are going to have a phone put in, so that when these stupid jobs come up I can ring and talk to you, love.'

Within 2 weeks we had our phone.

*****

41

The day was a Saturday and my work sheet read, 3 pm start, pick up at 5 pm at the Royal Medical Corp, Vauxhall, behind the Tate Gallery, and transfer to Aldershot, the Medical Head Quarters, wait and return.

We left London on time and the sergeant in charge of the outing asked me to join them if I so wished. I gave my thanks but said that I would stick with the tea from the cookhouse. We arrived about 90 minutes later and the sergeant pointed out the cookhouse, told me to let the people there know who I was and they would give me tea and a sandwich. I thanked them and watched the group walk into the Sergeants' Mess.

I parked the coach and made my way to the cookhouse where there was just one person on duty. I told them that I had just dropped the London Medical group at the Sergeants' Mess and that the sergeant had told me to ask kindly for tea and a sandwich. The cook said that there would be no problem and he would do that for me when he had just finished what he was doing.

After about 5 minutes my sandwich was just arriving when in comes the big fat camp Duty Sergeant, walks up to me and shouts in my ear, 'What the f*** hell are you doing in this Mess?'

I stood up and told my story but the response was still, 'Get the f*** hell out right now.'

I called across my thanks to the cook and strolled back to my coach. Sitting inside, looking across at the Sergeants' Mess an idea came to me. However I thought I might have further problems with this duty sergeant so had better inform the sergeant who I had left in the Mess, as to all about 'Big Mouth'. I entered the Sergeants' Mess and told the sergeant what had been going on.

He said to me, 'There is always one pratt to ruin the night. Have a pint.'

I said I would just have a shandy, and that's what I did.

Afterwards, sitting in my coach, the centre door opened. I jumped up to see it was 'Big Mouth' and shouted to him, 'Get off Fatso, this coach is private, your boundary is my step.'

I slammed shut the coach door, now guess what Fatso did next? He was that brave that he fetched 3 more heavy weights with him.

He said, 'Can we be friendly and have a drink outside this coach? Let's forget the silly talk we have had.'

'You must think I was born on a Christmas tree,' I replied, 'I step off this coach, have one mouthful of hard alcohol, then you and your 3 monkeys get stuck into me and pour drink all over me, and then report me to the civvy police to get me nicked. Look Fatso, you have made this problem, you can now sort it out.'

I then started the coach up, pulled away and drove back to Peckham. I thought about the nice bunch of guys who were enjoying their night away, but knew that if I had stepped off the coach I would have been attacked and finally arrested.

I wondered, 'Will I get the sack in the morning?'

In the army they sing 'Bless them all,' but on my way home I was singing, 'F*** them all, especially the Fat one.'

I arrived back at Peckham at about 11 pm and when I reached home told Betty about the events. I was a bit worried about the group coming out of the Mess and finding no coach waiting.

The next morning I set off for work at 7 am and was about 50 yards from the depot when I heard Charlie Banfield shouting like a mad man. 'I could lose all my coach services, the Isle of Grain contract!' Anyone would have thought I had just shot the Prime Minister. Now I knew I had upset Mr Banfield. About 5 yards from the depot I started singing, and that's how I entered the doors. Then the fat hit the pan.

Not 'Harry!' but 'Benton, come here!'

I walked over to him and he said, 'What the bloody hell went on last night at Aldershot? I've had a phone call that the coach left the camp and did not return to pick up the party and bring them back to London. What happened?'

I said to Mr Banfield, 'What do you pay me for? OK, you pay me to drive a vehicle, correct?'

He was looking at me and wondering what the hell I was talking about.

'To drive, correct?'

He nodded yes.

'Not to become some fat overweight Sergeant's punch bag, with a back up of 3 more heavy weights?'

I then told Mr Banfield the whole true story of that Saturday night. Afterwards he said that the CO in London wanted to get to the bottom of this mess, so I was to go over to the Royal Medical Corp for 10 am that day to see him.

My mate, Big Fred came with me for support and on arriving at the London Offices I saw the sergeant that I had left stranded the previous evening. I apologised to him and told him the whole story. He said that he had already told the CO that I had refused a drink, wanting only a cup of tea from the cookhouse. Then, as I entered the CO's office, Fatso himself came out, I just gave him a dirty look. The CO listened to what I had to say. I told him that I did not drink and drive as death came too quickly, without me adding to it by drinking. The CO told me that he would call Mr Banfield and waive any costs, and apologised for me having had a bad night.

The year was 1962. I was just leaving Banfield Garage when Mr Banfield called out, 'Harry, you are driving a bus tomorrow on a film set. Here is your ticket.'

The ticket read, 'Pick up in Earls Court Road at 7.30 am, then take the film crew to the Upminster and Dagenham area, wait and return.' Some film sets I had been on had been to advertise a soap powder or toothpaste so I was able to get away early. But on a film job the crew may have to take many shots to get the right one.

The next day I was waiting outside the door number, 15 minutes early, so I rang the doorbell and a lovely lady opened the door.

'Are you the driver?' she asked.

I nodded.

'Great,' she said, 'we will bring down the equipment.'

44

The traffic was getting very thick in Earls Court Road, as in those days it was 2 way traffic, and this flat was nearly opposite Earls Court Underground Station. London traffic was very heavy, bumper to bumper, and if the motorways had not been built we would have come to a stop long ago. We just threw the equipment onto the bus and drove off.

As we travelled along the Embankment, the chap in charge said, 'Driver, as you go along Cannon Street, on the corner of King William Street, you will see another person we are to pick up. His name is Michael Caine, so look out for him.'

I arrived in Cannon Street and as we passed Cannon Street Station started to look for this actor named Michael Caine.

I saw him on the corner, slid back my cab window and said, 'Michael Caine?'

'Yes.'

'Hop in.'

Driving along the old A13 route, I was told to look for the Four Oaks Café as we passed near Fords of Dagenham. After a few minutes I spotted it and pulled in. The car park for this café was full of potholes, so I drove with care so as not to damage the springs on the bus. Over the years, the heavy vehicles had made holes in the surface of the car park and the owners had just filled them with asphalt, and then when it rained and the trucks were back in the car park they just pushed the asphalt back down into the holes, therefore creating them again.

I climbed out of the cab and walked around to the back of the bus. Andrew, the person in charge, said, 'Harry, you and Michael go into the café and have some breakfast.'

We did so and while Michael studied the menu I was searching for the cheapest there. I ordered mine but then Michael said, 'I have left my money indoors.'

'Don't worry,' I said, 'I'll pay,' and I did.

When you sit with a top professional like Michael, you feel and see the difference with these actors. People would say to me that Michael Caine would be a big actor, and he is. *Well done Sir Michael Caine.*

But we must not forget the other top actor on the bus that day, Bryan Pringle. Bryan who? Remember the film Saturday Night/Sunday Morning? Some of you will be a little young to remember this film, but some of you will remember it with Albert Finney and Rachell Roberts. The story of the film was that Albert Finney was a spiv and was making love to Rachell Roberts, while poor old Bryan Pringle was her husband. His 2 brothers who were in the army saw that Albert Finney was up to no good with Rachell Roberts and gave Albert Finney a good beating. Although this film was only in black and white, it was still a good film.

The film set we were travelling to was 'Top Deck'. It's the story of a coloured guy from the good old USA, falling in love with a conductress. Instead of flying planes, this guy took off after this young ticket collector.

Michael Caine was only on set for 3 days.

Well, now that Michael Caine wasn't around, Andrew was looking for another actor but was not having much luck. So Harry, yes yours truly, was asked to do the part. So now you know the reason why the film did not get any Oscars or credits, in fact had you heard of the film 'Top Deck' until you read this book?

To fill up the bus Andrew used all the staff as they would not actually be seen in the film, and I was asked to be one of those getting on the bus to buy a ticket. The camera started rolling, shooting the passengers' hands as they bought tickets, but when they got to me the cameraman shouted, 'Stop the film, it's no good, Harry's hands look black in the camera. It now looks like we have 2 black guys on this bus.'

So I was kicked off my own bus! But it was good fun and the group were great. At night we used the back streets of any area that we came across for filming. The film took about 3 weeks in all to shoot.

When it was finished Andrew threw a party at his flat in Earls Court Road. Many unknown actors turned up, but over the years I have often seen a face and remembered them from that party. People like, Mr Dudley Sutton, who was there and I spoke to him.

I later received a telegram informing me that 'Top Deck' was being shown at the Film Festival at Southbank, and Betty and myself went along to see it.

Michael Caine went off the make 'Zulu' and many months later my family had a good laugh when Harry Secombe was on TV dressed as a Zulu. When the film came to our area Betty, Tony and myself went to see it. Tony tried to say something but I hushed him until the intermission.

'What do you want to know?' I asked Tony.

He replied, 'Which one of the Zulus was Harry Secombe?'

Betty and I rolled up, kids are funny.

Late during 1962 I was called to the office and Mr Banfield said to me. 'Harry, I want you to do the Dog Service, which is twice a week. The first race starts at 7.30 pm and the last race is 9.30 pm.' The Service route was from the George pub, which ran off Rushey Green and Lewisham High Street, down into Lewisham High Street, over into Lewisham Road, into Greenwich South Street and round into Romney Road. Then down Trafalgar Road, through Blackwall Tunnel, around the one way system, over Silvertown Bridge, turn right down Silvertown Way and onto the Dog Track. I said I would do it.

The same old faces would climb on to the coach each time. At first it was the same number of people each time, then word got around and I was left with just 6 empty seats on the coach. When the race was over I would ensure I got to my coach first, as there would be people who worked in the area looking for just a ride home for which I charged them 2 shillings, which in today's money is 10p. But it would not be just the 6 I took, but *26* standing. If I saw a police car I would shout, 'Squat down, police!' so as the police could not see them standing up.

Then I made the biggest mistake you could make; I broke my trust with a good man. Mr Banfield trusted me, but I got greedy and the gambling had a grip on me. When I filled in the paperwork for the trip I would put down 29 passengers, when in fact I had carried 39, and never told him about those who stood on the return journey. Mr Banfield became suspicious and put a 'spot' on my coach – a private Dick Tracy. A few days later I was called to his office where he asked me about the numbers on my coach. I stuck to my story, but I had broken his trust and I felt gutted over this.

Mr Banfield said to me, 'Harry, you are a bloody fool,' and I was.

I swore never to break my word again, or to rob an employer. When I think of it, my work rate was the best. If I moaned about an extra job, I would have forgotten about it the next day. The Banfield family were good, the son Michael was a laugh, in fact I ruined the whole friendship. Therefore during the early part of 1963 I left Banfield and went to work for Bloomfield Coaches.

During my first days of working for Bloomfields I was told I would be away for the night. I thought to myself, 'Here we go again, the Banfield trot. Out with nowhere to sleep,' but I was wrong. Mr Wallis said there was a party to pick up at the Strand Palace Hotel at 1.30 pm, and to take them to a hotel just outside Southampton (sorry, I've forgotten the name of the hotel, but will describe it later).

I said to Mr Wallis, 'Can I pop home for my overnight bag?'

He replied, 'Take my car, it's parked just over there.'

I called in at home, but Betty was not in, so I just left a note to let her know where I was off to, and then returned to the yard.

At 1.15 pm I was waiting outside the Strand Palace Hotel and some gentlemen from Esso came out, I took their overnight bags and placed them in the rear boot. We moved off bang on time.

Someone called out, 'Which way are you going driver?'

I replied, 'Towards Guildford, stopping for a coffee at Hindhead, the Devil's Punch Bowl. Gentlemen, if you have never seen the Punch Bowl it is worth stopping for.' The Devil's Punch Bowl is a massive hole in the ground, and to put my thinking cap on is about half a mile across; the view is well worth a stop.

We got through the London traffic and onto our route, arriving at Hindhead at about 3 pm. After coffee and a stroll to the Bowl for the view I said that we ought to be making tracks. Now, before setting off I would always check the fuel, oil, tyres, spare, jack and the bit, but obviously the fitters had not done their bit. As I went to start the coach the battery just went 'click', and I knew I had a flat battery. I lifted the centre panel and saw that the battery was full of corrosion.

I said, 'Gentlemen please. I have some good new and some bad news, which do you want first?'

'The bad news is that the battery is 'zip', and the good news is that I have some exercise for you. Get out and push!'

They rolled up laughing, but they pushed and got it started.

The boss man asked, 'Will we get to the hotel?'

I said, 'Yes, and I will have a new battery on this coach for tomorrow.'

When we reached the hotel – I would say this was built in Portland Stone and looked Georgian, about 18th century – I said, 'Gentlemen, please grab your own bag so you know you have it, I'm off to see that this coach is in running order for tomorrow.'

My first move was to contact the Maitre D' at the hotel, as I needed information on many things, those being a tool box, a shop selling batteries and the best taxi service in the area. Many thanks to the staff of that hotel as I was pulling away in the coach the next morning at 9 am.

The battery cost me £9 and on returning to the yard I showed the bill to Mr Wallis. To cut this short, he was a great guy, Mr Wallis added a '1' in front of the '9' on the bill to make it read £19. That is what I call *finesse*. He had had not one phone call from me regarding this problem, and so he gave me this large tip of £10. I then knew that I would be able to work side by side with him at Bloomfields.

The early days of 1963 were very cold. I would get up in the mornings, make my way to the kitchen and turn on the gas

49

tap to warm up this small room. By the time Betty and Tony got up the kitchen was nice and warm for them.

One morning I did just this and had my back to the gas stove, when out of the corner of my eye I saw the cupboard door's paint work had flames flickering on it. Then I knew *I* was on fire too. My pyjamas were alight and were starting to burn my back. In a panic I ripped off my pyjamas and of course then my hands were burning. I cried out for Betty to help me and then realised that Tony was there and saw the terror in his eyes. He screamed out to me, 'My Daddy, my Daddy!' It felt worse to hear that than to feel the burning in my hands. Betty slipped on my shoes, trousers and camel coat, covered my hands with a towel and I rushed to East Dulwich Hospital just a few minutes away. As I was running the coldness was penetrating the towels and attacking my hands, it felt as though the hospital was miles away.

I rushed into Casualty and a doctor said, 'Can I help you?'

'Please, I have burnt my hands and am in a lot of pain.'

'Right,' he said, 'I'll give you a dose of morphine.'

The morphine took about 10 minutes to work and then it just felt like pins and needles. He swabbed my hands and then each finger was strapped up. This meant that I would need help with everything, even someone to unzip my flies to go to the loo. Ha!

I contacted the Bloomfield office, told them of the story and that I would pop in to see them. For the bus fare Betty put some change in the top pocket of my camel coat, so it was no problem for the bus conductor to collect his fare. At work in the drivers' room they all thought it was a laugh until it was time for me to go home.

Before leaving I needed to pay a visit to the gents, so I asked, 'Who wants to do the honours for me and unzip me?'

At once all the drivers had turned deaf.

'That's nice isn't it?' I said to one of the drivers, 'I will just have to ask your wife who works in the offices.'

'OK,' said the driver, Reg Ainsworth, 'I don't want my wife to see your John Thomas, or else she will be saying to me, why don't you eat the same as Harry?'

But it was all in good fun.

Three weeks later I was back on the road and doing the tours.

One day Bernie Wallis drove into our yard and this beautiful woman got out of his car. I thought, 'What cornflakes box did this beauty come out of?' Bernie beckoned me over to them; now I was walking like a zombie, I just could not take my eyes off her, she was world class.

Bernie said, 'Harry, meet Miss Great Britain, Joy Black.'

I started to stutter, 'Can I help you?' Yes, that's what I said, 'Can I help you?' I felt like a dick head.

Bernie said, 'Harry, you can drive my car and pick up Joy whenever she calls you.'

OK yes, I would do that I thought licking my lips.

'And another thing,' Bernie said, 'there is a coach firm down in Folkestone, and I want you to take their brand new coach on the Brighton Coach Rally. The coach will be here next week.'

So there I was, looking after Joy *and* taking a coach on the Brighton Rally. Good things usually come in threes and 2 had just arrived, Joy Black and the fact that I was taking this brand new coach for the Rally.

The coach arrived from Folkestone and I must say it did look good. The coach was maroon, a dark purplish red colour and I must say it did shine. It was only a small 18/20 seater so it would not win top prize, but I could enter for the Best Dressed Uniformed Driver, and that was my aim.

Then came a call to pick up Joy Black, so I rushed over to her hotel just off Sussex Gardens, W2. She wanted to do a dummy run through the back streets to Biggin Hill. Off we went, back roads to Crystal Palace Parade, down Anerley Hill, across over into Elmers End Road, and at that point Joy gave one big scream, nearly frightening me to death.

'What's up?' I said.

She replied, 'I've got no stockings on.'

'God almighty, I thought you had had a heart attack.'

We were just reaching some shops and I sent Joy off into the nearest ladies shop. She came out waving a small package and then started to pull the stockings out. She then started to roll down the top of the stocking and on reaching the car, Joy opened the door and started to put it on. I just stared out of my window, the passing traffic was hooting and there were wolf whistles.

I said to her, 'Joy, you will cause an accident if you are not careful,' but I could not stop laughing. This girl was so unbelievable but great fun, and I will also add, a very intelligent person with a good outlook on life.

Joy opened the Brighton Coach Rally and I won the Best Dressed Uniformed Driver just as I had wanted. She also opened the Biggin Hill Air Show and many other things. Joy was good to work with, and the God's honest truth, there was never any hanky panky between Joy and myself.

Today, Joy lives with her husband and is writing a book about her life called '**I Am Still Here**'. Good luck Joy!

As you read this next story, you must read between the lines, I am approaching the story in this way.

I was working for Bloomfield Coaches, and the company had a contract with a large European company. Our part was to meet the groups at the airport, transfer them to a London hotel and then do the London, Windsor and Stratford-upon-Avon tours, 5-star tours, the best. The Registered Tour Guide was Major Battcock and his wife Jackie was also a Registered Guide, and whilst doing the tours I became very friendly with them.

During the early part of the summer of 1963 I was doing some shopping in Rye Lane, Peckham. I was busy daydreaming and looking in the shop windows when a head rested upon my head and a voice said, 'Watcha mate!'

I looked around and saw it was Moses. I said to him, 'I see you are slumming it the same as I.' Meaning that we were not doing our shopping in Regents Street. I asked him how his mum and dad were. Then Moses turned to me and said, 'I might have a driving job for you, would you be interested in it?'

I said, 'If you was asking me now I would say 'yes', but ask me again when you are ready.'

'OK Harry.'

I was driving a coach and my tour guide Major Battcock asked me, 'Would you like to become a Registered London Tourist Guide?'

I said, 'I would jump at it.'

'Well,' he said, 'I will put your name down for the interview and if you are lucky the course starts at the end of September this year.

Betty, Tony and myself had decided to have a holiday and had booked at Butlins, Skegness for the last week in August, so that I could be back in time for my interview for the Tourist Guide. At the same time Betty's Mum was unwell.

A good friend of mine, Nobby Goswark from Peckham, an ex-marine, said to me, 'Harry are you going on holiday?'

'Yes,' I replied.

'Well mate, take my car.' This man had just bought a brand new car for £500 and now he was letting me have the car for the week.

Time moved on, and one day I was coming out of the flat to cross over Quorn Road when a black car pulled up beside me. Out jumped Moses and told me that the driving job was ready for me.

'Sorry Moses, but the Tourist Board want me to take a course on London, also Betty's Mum is not well.'

'OK Harry, don't worry about it, I will cover the job.'

Then I heard a train had been robbed of just over £2 million, and I thought, ' I wonder if?'

We were all packed ready for our holiday and I was taking Tony to catch the number 37 bus to Peckham to pick up the car. I then saw Moses and I asked him if that had been the driving job he had offered me, and he nodded.

'Let me take you anywhere you like, I have my friend's car and I will run you anywhere.'

'No,' said Moses, 'I will be OK.' That was the last time I saw him

*If the Major had not put me down for the tourist's job I may have been tied up in **The Great Train Robbery**.*

I was called to the Queens House in St James for the interview with Major Battcock and another 10 important people. I was asked how well I knew London, Canterbury, Stratford, Oxford, and city after city. By now I was silently thanking Banfield Coaches and the other coach work I had done. I named the bus routes from Piccadilly to South London and the Victoria area, and made a mental note to study the buildings very hard. I was smartly dressed as I had been told that this would help me. They then told me that I would be contacted by post.

On returning to the yard I asked if I could phone my Betty to put her in the picture about the interview. I also said that if the letter gave me the all clear on the course I would have long weekends off walking the streets of London.

I arrived home one afternoon, my phone was ringing, and it was the boss of Violour Coaches. He said he was stuck for a driver that evening, a 6 pm pick up at the bottom of Kingsway and the Aldwych, at the main office for ATV. I asked him to give me 2 minutes and I would ring him back, this was just to ensure that it was a genuine call. This I did and accepted the job for that evening.

I popped up to the back streets of East Dulwich to pick up the old coach and said, 'I want cash payment now, not tomorrow.' He paid me, told me to return the coach to the road outside when the job was finished and to drop the coach keys back through the letterbox.

I returned home, did another hour's work on my book and then got ready for this evening trip. In those days it would only take 40 minutes from leaving home to reaching the pick up point, but in today's traffic it takes much, much longer. Betty arrived home just as I was about to leave, I told her that Violour Coaches needed me urgently and would see her much later, and then I was gone.

I arrived about 5.50 pm outside the pick up point and the group all emerged to get on the coach. I spoke to the man carrying a clip board, who told me we were off to Deptford, near the River Thames, to a place called (if I remember right) Longshore or Foreshore. As I looked up I was dumb struck. There were 2 top singers of the day, that smashing guy Matt Monro and Dennis Lotus, and the woman, I am not sure, but I think it was Cleo Lane.

As I climbed into my seat Dennis Lotus said, 'Driver, if you get fed up with driving, Matt will drive for you.'

I stood up and said jokingly, 'Ladies and Gentlemen, I will do the driving and let Matt do the singing,' and we were off on our way to Deptford.

This entire trip was for a TV show that was to be on our television within the next 2 weeks. It was a great night, and very good company. What gratuities did I get for this job? Well, it was a *big elbow* job, meaning I got nothing, but Matt Monro made it for me, I felt like I had a front row seat for it.

REGISTERED TOURIST GUIDE OF LONDON

The Tourist Guide course started at 7.30 pm at the Queens House in St James's off Piccadilly. There were about 25 people on the course from all walks of life - taxi drivers, actors, coach drivers and bus inspectors. The tutor was Mr Charles Pearson who, I may add, was very good. It ran twice a week and you were expected to walk the streets of London at weekends, and visit all the well-known buildings. You would be asked questions about history, arts, Kings and Queens, and prominent years in English history, so this information all needed finding and reciting to memory. Because of all the time this would take I had to say goodbye to my job with Bernie Wallis at Bloomfields, and just found the odd job here and there to keep cash coming in at home.

The course was for 2 hours at a time, and afterwards I would catch a taxi from outside Queens House, over to the south side of Westminster Bridge to outside London County Hall, where on the corner by the Edward and Alexandra Hospital was my bus stop, and I would be indoors about 20 minutes later. After a few months I would be at home writing on a subject and the next thing that I knew would be Betty waking me up at about 4 am, telling me to try to get some sleep in bed before I started work. I was driving a truck for a firm in Peckham at that time.

One evening after finishing the course I stopped a taxi outside the Queens House, to find the cab driver very excited and talking fast.

'Have you heard about President Kennedy?' he asked.

'No, what has been going on?' I replied.

'The President has been shot and they've rushed him to hospital.'

Indoors again, Betty put on the TV whilst I made tea, but there was no further news that evening. The next morning we heard that this *great* President had died. I say *great,* because he stood up to Cuba and the USSR and made our world safe.

The day came for the oral examination, which I knew I would do well at, it was the written examination that would be my downfall if any, and then the letter arrived telling me I had failed. A group of us all met and talked about this and that, and I knew then that I had been a fool, as I did not know about chronological, meaning to arrange in date order.

Do you remember a TV comedy, 'Duty Free'? It was the story of 2 couples on a Spanish holiday; one husband fancied another one's wife. If you remember the little heavily built guy who was the Spanish waiter named Carlos? Well his real name was Carlos Douglas and he was on the course with me, and he passed the exam. In 1996 my present wife Margaret and I met Carlos for dinner in the West End and had a good night out.

After failing the course I was taken sick, but not because I felt upset at the failure, I could not understand what it was, it was something I had never had before. I went to my doctor whose surgery was very close by – I'd changed from the German doctor to this Canadian one, only for the fact that this one was closer, if you threw a stone you would hit it – and told him I had a sore throat.

He told me, 'Have 2 weeks off work.'

'You are joking, doctor? I've just lost time and money doing the London Tourist Course, which I failed, and now my family and I have no money and I'll loose even more because I'm sick.' So I decided to take just the one week off.

The following week I went back to the doctor and said, 'I cannot walk, I have to lift my legs with my arms and I feel weak.'

All he could say was to have another week off.

I went back to work and thank God I did. It was a Saturday morning and I was working for Bernie Wallis at the Mandeville Hotel. It had offices on the first floor, a nice hotel with about 90 rooms. Mr Wallis had started up a new company called Safhire International, a company with cars and coaches just off Oxford Street near Manchester Square. The company manager was Shirley, one hell of a great girl, a top boss who knew her job backwards.

That morning Shirley asked me to pop to Bell and Coopers, the chemist in Wigmore Street, so I did just that.

An old gentleman in there said to me, 'It looks like your bad ankle is making you ill. I would advise you to go to the local hospital.'

I went back and told Shirley what the old gent had said and she told me to go. I drove to Kings College Hospital near Camberwell and parked by the front step, you could in those days. I had to wait for a few people in front of me to be seen and then the doctor called my number. I told him my problems and he told me to go into the next cubicle, get undressed and he would be along to see me soon. I did just that and remember looking at my watch and seeing 1.30 pm as I lay on the bed.

The next thing I remember was waking up and the time was 6.30 pm. Thank God it was the same day, because someone could have wheeled me off to the mortuary thinking I was 'brown bread' – dead. I called out to a nurse and told her that I had been there since 1.30 pm and nobody had seen me yet. It wasn't just one doctor I got then, but 3 rushing around me.

I tried asking to use the phone to contact my wife but they just said, 'Do not worry Mr Benton, we are doing a top medical check on you.'

Then one of the doctors said, 'Sorry Mr Benton, you will be here for 6 weeks, you have rheumatic fever.'

I managed to phone Betty and she rushed over with my toiletries. They put me in Stork Ward, what a ward to stick me in. Betty was pregnant at the time, surely the name was more apt for her condition!

Before I was taken to Stork Ward I told the doctor that I could not have penicillin. When the doctor asked the reason, I told him that it attacked my throat, and he said that I would be all right. By my bedside was a large pill, and when I asked if it was penicillin was told it was not. During that night I felt very ill and called to the night staff, they checked me over and started whispering amongst themselves. I was glad when morning eventually came. I asked the chap in the next bed to me if I could use his mirror, and that's when I saw the whole of my throat was covered in big red spots. I felt that I could have died because of some nut of a doctor that didn't listen to people.

The head doctor was making his ward rounds, with all his 'pups' following in little white coats. The next bit I'm going to tell I found very interesting. The chap on my right hand side had a tracheotomy, which is an incision in the air passage that has been blocked. I listened to what the head doctor had to say. He asked his students how they could tell without the use of a x-ray that this man had a bad chronic chest? They did not say a word; it was beginning to remind me of the old doctors' films, the answer was that the patient's fingers would end up bent over at the tips like claws. When the man who was sick was asked a question, the doctor put his finger on the pipe that lead down to his throat, and when he spoke it sounded like a train coming off the track. *I knew that sound well, as when I was a stoker I saw and heard many a train in the shunt yards come off the track.*

Now it was my turn. The head doctor asked how I felt, and I replied, 'Bloody rough.'

'Why?'

'Just look at my throat,' which he did, 'I told that dick head that I was not to have *penicillin*.' By now I was shouting at him.

The head doctor turned to his students and said, 'When you are told by somebody that they cannot take medicine that can harm them, just do not let them have it. Mr Benton could have died.'

They then moved to the bed on my left. The chap was a London taxi driver from Brixton, with blood problems, and that's as much as he was willing to say.

Two or 3 hours later some more doctors visited me, one of them was the Queen's doctor - the other doctors told me that fact, and that he was the top one in London. He told me that I was a very lucky chap and had what they call 'athletic heart', which is a very strong heart, a 3 beater rather than the normal 2 beater, which had saved my life. He said that the cure for the rheumatic fever was aspirin taken with lots of water, and rest.

Most of the fellows in the ward were there for long periods, so the taxi driver chap and I kept a book on the first visitor through the door. Now remember Betty was pregnant and showing well, and that helped her to be first through the door. First through would win the kitty, well we did not win *every* night. If it was a tie we would be given the kitty as the baby was through first, we did have some laughs.

Mr Wallis came in to see me and was good to me as he brought in my pay packet now and then. Once I was better I gave him my full support with overtime and extra weekends.

On 7 November 1964 Betty started having bad pains with the baby. Doctor Common called for an ambulance and when it was leaving I shouted out, 'What hospital are we going to?'

He said, 'Follow me.'

I had an old banger of a car and it must have looked silly, chasing this ambulance up Doggy, through to Walworth Road, to Westminster Bridge, turn right into York Road and to the Edward and Alexandra Hospital. This was the hospital where my sister Ellen had been born 40 years earlier. However the baby kept us waiting until the 8 November, and then Betty named him David.

At the beginning of 1965 the company moved from the hotel to Crawford Street, not far away. We lost Shirley, who moved to another company down Bayswater Road, and soon after that Mr Wallis went as well.

I was busy working hard on my new London Tourist Guide Course, being held at Bolts Lock in the old City of London, just off Fleet Street. Let me just ask you a question. How many roads in the City of London? There are none; in the old roman square mile of London the vehicle routes are all streets!

On this course were a group of kind people, if, like myself, you got a bit out of depth, there was always someone to jump in and help. The best was Maurice Pike, our teacher. He told me to write about the history of buildings like Hampton Court Palace. The following week I handed in my work and within minutes Mr Pike was throwing it back to me and shouting, 'Rubbish! do it all again.' He told the class that I had the best pass for the oral examination during my last course, but I failed on the written examination, so they were to all help me get through.

The new boss at our company was John Wilkinson, only a kid but clever. It wasn't long before I moved with Bernie Wallis. He had started a new company with some hotel owners, called Plaza Travel, operating from Craven Road, W2. Bernie let me have the time off that I needed, to work hard and not to let Mr Pike and myself down again.

Whilst on this course I got friendly with a taxi driver named Stan Payne who lived in Crayford, Kent. We were having a chat when Stan mentioned that there was a house for sale right opposite where he lived. Two weeks previous to this I had had the local council round to see how rough it was for us living in just one little bedroom, so I was after another place with space. I asked Stan the price of the house for sale, and he said £4999, it had 3 bedrooms, good sized garden which faced south, which told you that the sun shined into your back garden the whole time.

When I reached home I told Betty of this chat. It was a Saturday, and a local lad named Goldie, called on me to go to Catford Dog Races.

I said to him, 'Sorry Goldie, but I only have 3 quid on me.'

'Come on Harry, try your luck.'

Well, I went to Catford Dogs. There was a double up race, in which you have to correctly give the first and second dogs in the first race, then the winnings go on the first and second in the next race. So, I placed my bets and hoped for the best. Over 3000 tickets were bought, which was not bad. My dogs were in traps 4 and 6, and they came through, there was a photo finish and my dogs got it. Out of 3000 tickets only 25 won, because the favourite was an outsider. I then placed a bet on the favourite to beat the outsider, mine being in traps 1 and 4, and they came up. This time I held the only winning ticket. My winnings that evening totalled £364 which was good money in those days. I gave the lads £5 each out of my winnings and the cheque for £300 was in my back pocket.

In class, Mr Pike was pleased with my homework, he could see that I desperately wanted to get through the examination this time. I loved the Tower of London, and I had a way of pulling the people to the private site of the scaffold. I would beckon to them and say, 'Come here! Come here! You can feel the dead people who died on this site.' As people gathered around I would tell them the stories of each one, and then the gratuities would start because I finished with a laugh saying, '..so do not forget and tip me tonight.'

The day of the test came, it was at Caxton Hall, and Mr Pike wished us all well. Boy, was I feeling bad, so did some deep breathing and it did help.

The paperwork was 60 quick questions to do in 30 minutes, then about 6 essays to write, with a choice of 2 for each subject. One of the choices was to write about the new building of the Barbican or the life of Sir Thomas Moore. I chose to do about Moore, and it turned out that I was the only one to do this.

Afterwards, we all met in the local pub to talk about the exam. It was Mr Pike that I was looking for, because he was one great man, a walking knowledge book of London, who had pushed and shouted me through that examination. When he entered he told me he was most impressed that I had chosen to write about Moore.

Three weeks later, Mr Pike informed me that I had **passed.**

So there I was having had no education as such, but I had just learned that I was now a Registered London Tourist Guide. I would not let the Tourist Board down, I would give the tourists *more* than they paid for, and I did just that. Over the years I gave the Jewish tourist Bevis Marks synagogue in the City, and on the Stratford tour would always put in Bladon to include Sir Winston Churchill's grave. A few drivers would moan about any extras I wanted to include, but I looked at it this way. Tourists could have travelled many thousands of miles, so what was wrong with going one extra mile up the road for the tourist, to sell to them the beauty and history of our country. When they went home and were asked how they had been treated, I liked to hear them say, 'Just great!' I didn't want to hear moaning about the tour. Help make Britain great and just be happy with the tourists.

Now I had my Registered Tourist Guide Badge and was very proud of all the work I had put in to achieve this as it was all worth it.

I told Bernie Wallis that I would always cover his tours first but that I had to now make all the hard work pay for itself, and he understood.

Stan Payne from Crayford also passed. Things were now beginning to move for that house we had seen in Crayford. Betty and I had taken a Sunday trip to see it and she had instantly fallen in love with it. I had contacted the Greater London Council Housing Department, had a meeting with them and was awarded a 100% mortgage. So now we just had to wait and see if we could beat any other people who may be interested.

There were 2 ways of doing the City Tour; a licensed company would stick to the route of their licence. That would be to leave the WestEnd at 2 pm and make their way to St Paul's Cathedral. This is a must, if anyone comes to London please make sure you visit this Cathedral, it is full of history, but remember it is also a place of God. Then the tour would take you to the Tower of London to tour at your own pace and then return to your hotel by taxi, or stick with the tour guide, seeing this and that, including the Crown Jewels, and the tour would finish about 5 to 5.30 pm. But remember I am talking about the sixties and we would do our own thing.

It depended on the time of the year, and from June to September I would alter the tour so that our tourists got their monies worth. I would do the City Tour in the morning, making sure we were back for the Changing of the Guards at the Palace, then in the afternoon the tour of Westminster, because this way you missed all the hustle and bustle of the crowds.

We would leave about 8.45 am and drive through the first part of the City, 'This is where the money is made.' Then to the West End, 'This is where the money is spent.' At St Paul's Cathedral I liked to take the group down to the crypt. Now that does hold a great deal of our history; Nelson, Wellington, Wren, and many other famous people. From there we were off to the Tower of London, touring this in the morning was great. Many of the tours were with Unitours of New York and they were a Jewish company. I made contacts with the Rabbi so that we could visit the Bevis Marks Synagogue. This is the oldest synagogue in London, built after the resettlement in 1656. However, Oliver Cromwell bought the Jewish people back into England, wanting money to fight the Royals. Around Soho in the WestEnd is another synagogue, near Marble Arch.

By now we had bought the house in Crayford, Kent for a price of £4,999.

A train ride from London to Crayford in Kent took between 25 and 45 minutes depending on the number of stations it stopped at, during the rush hour it would take the 45 minutes. Well, today the train was on the 45 minute run, the time was about 1.15 pm and I had just finished a morning City Tour of London. The group had come from New York and were with Unitours, they were Jewish and were staying at the Piccadilly Hotel. My train was just pulling into New Cross Station and I began to think about that morning's tour, my mind was retracing the events to see if I had left anything out of the tour which could have been interesting to them.

I was always early in arriving to meet the people wishing to travel with the best Registered Tourist Guide in London. I did not cut any corners, in fact I added to the tour. We, the people of the UK and the Tourist Board wanted the tourists to come back again.

I looked around the hotel lobby to find the travel desk where the group was all waiting. A travel desk would be set aside for this purpose, with the name of the group marked up on a board. I greeted the group, who replied and followed me out of the hotel once they had grabbed their coats. I found the driver in his coach and quickly discussed with him the route I wished to follow; it is much more professional for the driver to know the route rather than myself having to direct him all the way.

The group was now aboard and we set off up Regents Street – named after the Prince Regent, and designed by an architect by the name of Nash. If you walk up this street you will see the way it curves round to the right, this is because

64

Nash wanted to miss the area of Soho. Today, Soho is a very busy place with small markets and many shops and of a night time it has many adult clubs offering lots of fun if you like that way of life.

London is split into 2, the City of London where the money is made, and the WestEnd (where we are now) where the money is spent.

Along Oxford Street, with all the stores for ladies (and gents) to shop until they drop. Down into Kensington High Street, again full of shops. Now we could see Kensington Palace, and I would talk of Queen Victoria and Prince Albert. Queen Victoria was born in the Cube Room and it was here that this young lady was informed that she was Queen. A little way down the road is the Royal Albert Hall and across the road the Prince Albert Memorial. (This was the route taken by the funeral of Princess Diana leading to Westminster Abbey and of course Kensington Palace with the millions of flowers.)

Arriving at the Abbey I would tell my group many do's and don'ts before entering; no flash cameras, only whisper to each other, and it's a place of worship and prayers were being taken all the time. Edward the Confessor's shrine is there and above the Coronation Chair is a freeze of the life of Edward the Confessor. But look closely at the freeze and you will see a little pageboy is trying to steal money from Edward. The Abbey is a must of places to visit in London; it is full of our history.

Up to Buckingham Palace, built by the Duke of Buckinghamshire and the London home for our Queen and the Royal Family. Here we would see the Changing of the Guards, taking about 30 minutes for them to do their pass by.

Back to the hotel and it's finished.

It was another beautiful day, the sun was shining and I was outside the Londoner Hotel for another morning City Tour of London. Today I had a Japanese group to take around the WestEnd. We set off about 10 minutes late, and an interpreter explained to the group just what I was saying.

We arrived at Constitution Hill at about 11.15 am and the group left the coach to see the Changing of the Guards. It was just one week away from the Queen's Trooping of the Colours and Constitution Hill was packed with tourists. I remember seeing Robert Vaughan the actor from 'The Man From U.N.C.L.E.' on a corner being mobbed by the people.

The tour guides and drivers were all chatting away together, when a Japanese man approached me and started talking to me in Japanese. I thought he was going through the Japanese dictionary, I could not understand one word he said. Then his hands were on his stomach and I quickly said, 'Taxi? Cab? Rickshaw?' and with that word he nodded. I indicated to him to stay right there and not to move, then I carefully went into the road to flag down a cab. Within seconds I look around and he had gone.

I walked back looking for him and saw a group of guides and drivers all laughing. I walked up to them and asked if they had seen my Japanese man, and at the same time looked at what they were laughing at.

There was my man with his trousers down doing a *whoopsie* behind a plain tree, right beside the wall that surrounds Buckingham Palace and protects the Queen's gardens.

Well, I did not know where to look next. Then a big policeman came up and asked who was responsible for that person dropping his goods outside the Queen's home. I explained to the officer, and then the Japanese man came over and I called a cab to return him to his hotel to clean up. I told the cabby the name of the hotel and then returned to the group of guides and drivers, and the policeman.

I said to the policeman, 'Officer, if you are going to charge me for the Japanese whoopsie, then I will insist that you collect all the evidence that the man has left and bring it into court.' That comment produced a great deal of laughter.

One day I arrived back at Crayford Station and set off for home, I did not live far from the station. As I walked down my front steps I heard the phone ringing and quickly went to answer it so as not to loose the call. I was freelancing at the time, so all calls and letters were a must, it's money mate!

I picked up the phone and said, 'Benton here.'

A young lady replied, 'Harry, it's the Unitours desk in the Piccadilly Hotel, we have a Stratford Tour going tomorrow. Are you free?'

'Yes, I'm free tomorrow. Is it all booked and what time is lunch?'

'We have booked for 40 lunches at 1 pm at the White Swan in Stratford.'

'OK,' I said, 'see you for an 8 am start from the hotel.'

That night I told Betty of the next day's work and that I wouldn't get home until late. I told her, 'I will take Tony with me.' Tony was by now 10 years old. 'It will give him a break from school, but he will not lose anything, he will pick up some history in Oxford and in Stratford.'

The next morning Tony and I arrived at the Piccadilly Hotel at 7.30 am. Most people know that I have a neck (that means that I am not afraid to ask for this or that). So I went up to the Head Porter and said, 'I am taking the Unitours off to Stratford this morning, any chance of a cup of tea and toast in the main restaurant for my son and I?'

'That's OK mate, I'll let the Head Waiter know,' he said.

Just as we were going into the restaurant I walked into Cassius Clay (Muhammad or Mohammed Ali). He was there to box 'our Henry'. If any of my army pals are reading this book, they will know how I like to box; I was the 3rd Tank Champion. I said to him, 'Good morning,' and he just nodded.

Just after 8 am we set off, our route taking us along the M4 and off to Henley, up through Box, and a stop for coffee at the Chicken in the Basket at Bensons. Whilst on route I just gave them bits and pieces, not too much chat at this stage, just enough to let them know I hadn't fallen asleep.

We arrived at Oxford and went to Wadham College, this was the college I would cover on my tours, and we each had a particular college we covered. I pointed out that it was founded 1610 to 1613, and built by Wadhams. Christopher

67

Wren was one of its famous members and from its gardens you can see Rhodes House. Down just a few more yards is Keble College, which again is my college for the tours, with the famous painting 'The Light of the World' by Holman Hunt. After our tour of Keble College we drove on towards Stratford-upon-Avon. On the way we would visit the grave of a great man, Sir Winston Churchill at Bladon. Again this is a must, these people travelled thousands of miles and the grave was only one mile off our route. If you remember, his mother Jenny was half-American, and when I travelled with the Yanks, boy did they enjoy this short detour.

On arriving at Stratford-upon-Avon the coach stopped outside the hotel and I went inside to confirm lunchtime and menu. Then I nearly dropped dead. PORK was on the menu, and my group was Jewish. I went bonkers!

I said to the Head Waiter, 'Do something about the menu, we just *cannot* serve pork to a Jewish group. I will tell them you are running late but they can have a free drink with their meal.'

'Put it on the bill and I will sign it for you.'

I told the group there would be a small hold up with lunch but it would be ready for 1.15 pm. In the meantime we popped to Anne Hathaway's Cottage, as it was only 5 minutes away. Luckily there was no-one else there at the time and we were on the tour straight away finishing with photos outside, and then back for lunch arriving at 1.30 pm

Sitting down for lunch I was dead frightened as to what I would find on the menu now. I said in a high voice, 'Sorry we're late, but we are ready now.' I picked up the menu and it read 'veal'.

Somebody shouted out, 'Harry, what is veal?'

'It's a young calf and veal comes from the top of the back legs,' I said, holding my breath.

'Well, I'll try anything once,' the chap shouted back.

Whilst the group ate their lunch I tried to find out who had dropped this clanger, the hotel or the travel desk, and I was told it had been the travel desk back at the Piccadilly Hotel.

After lunch we completed the full tour of this historic town and then made our way home via Banbury. We stopped there for afternoon tea and Banbury cake, and I always stood up and gave them the nursery rhyme.

Ride a cock horse to Banbury cross, to see a fair lady on a white horse. With rings on her fingers and bells on her toes, she will have music wherever she goes.

As we reached the county town of Aylesbury in Buckinghamshire, I told the story of the Great Train Robbery in August 1963, but I left myself out of it. Come on, who would have believed that? I had just told the true events and for them to believe that I came close to being involved with it, sorry it's too much! I pointed out the courts where the 'over the top' sentence was handed out, and told them about the £2 million loss.

We arrived back at the Piccadilly Hotel at about 7.30 pm. Some had tickets booked for the theatre and had hoped for an earlier return to the hotel, the travel desk should not have sold the tickets knowing that the tour was a full day of England's countryside. There was nobody at the travel desk when we arrived, which again was wrong. What if somebody had need further help, if there had been an accident or somebody had fallen sick. So I saw them to the front desk to obtain their keys and Tony and myself then went home. I gave Tony £2 out of my tips.

It had been a good day, but could have been a real f*** up day.

By now I was well away, doing this tour and that tour, but trying to make a name for myself. I wanted this so that I could start asking my own price for a tour, then people would say how good I was.

One day I was called to Earls Court Road, to a small travel office. The manager asked me, 'Can you do a 5 day and 4 night trip through England into Scotland and back. There are 18 American passengers, starting next Monday and return

69

back on Friday night. The hotels are very good, they are 4-star. The group is known to each other and the tour must be very good, because if there are no problems we can then try to obtain a licence for this trip. That is why I wanted to see you in person, not by phone.'

'Who is the coach company?' I asked.

'Plaza Travel.'

Good old Bernie, he had put my name up front for this travel outfit and the tour. I took the job.

Monday came and I arrived to collect my passengers, some of them approached me for a chat, so I responded with, 'How do you like England?' and 'When do you return back to the good old USA?' The coach arrived early so I called out the names, collected the tickets and once I knew we had the correct number of passengers we were off. I told the group that they would see the things and places that they had paid for, but could they tell the travel agent that this was the best tour they had ever been on.

First stop was at Oxford where I showed them Wadham College, tying up the connection here with Sir Christopher Wren with their visit to London. Then we dashed off to Bladon to see Churchill's grave, up the road to Stratford-upon-Avon, a quick visit to the church and Shakespeare's birthplace. We then stopped for a snack to eat, and I made them laugh by telling them this had to be quick, they would eat that evening, but I wanted to fit in as much as I could for them on this trip. From Stratford it was then up to the Lake District where we stayed overnight looking over Lake Windermere. We all met for dinner at 8 pm where we talked about the trip and the history.

Day 2 began with a slow ride around the lakes, then out to Carlisle and Gretna Green. The Scottish piper was there, and I managed to confuse 2 of our married couples on the trip, by mixing them up and trying to marry them off again to the other partner. I did this to encourage people to mix and enjoy themselves, as I didn't like grumpiness on my trips. We arrived at Edinburgh that evening with time to spare. I went out for dinner with some people that I knew in Edinburgh; it gave me a short break from the group.

On Day 3 we left the hotel in Princess Street and made our way to Callander and Kilmohog Woollen Mills, for the group to buy any Scottish gifts they wanted. Then a drive through the Trossachs and down to Loch Lomond, and back over to Stirling Castle. I then told my story about the Battle of Bannockburn in 1314, as from this castle you could see the area that the battle took place. The Scots won.

At dinner that evening, I was seated alone and a gentleman and lady asked if they could join me.

'Sure,' I said, 'please take a pew.'

When they told me who they were I nearly fell off my seat, they were Jay Dermer, Mayor of the City of Miami, Florida and the lady was his secretary. The Mayor said that they had both had a great trip and that I must be worth a goldmine to the company. He then told me that he would like to present me with the Key to the Freedom of the City of Miami, I was dumbfounded.

On Day 4 our trip took us down to Galashiels, to the home of Sir Walter Scott. This was near Melrose Abby, where the heart of Robert the Bruce lays in the burial grounds. We had lunch in the Station Hotel in Newcastle, then drove around and down to York. We stopped here for a visit before travelling to our hotel for the night.

Our final day took us to Ripon, which is a city older than London itself is. The locals did say that they had a town cryer still in the city, but I do not know that for sure. Then it was back to London to finish the tour by Friday evening.

After the Mayor of Miami had handed me the Key to his City I thought, 'What will come next?' Well, it did not take long. A company known as Kingsway Travel, based in Kingsway in the City of London, phoned me and asked me to come in and see their Managing Director. Boy, I was there like a shot!

Our talk was about a company in Chicago called Cartan Tours, who wanted to run a 3 week tour of Ireland, Scotland, brushing the edge of Wales, and then England. These people would be paying for a 5-star service, so it was only the best for them. The route would take them through the best countryside in the United Kingdom and with full board. It would start in Shannon Airport, staying at the International Hotel, and I would have to be there for the night before the group arrived, as they would be arriving on a morning flight from Chicago. Then the Managing Director asked me if I had any questions.

I said, 'If I can better the tour with extra attractions on route, could I do this if I checked with you first?'

'OK,' he said, 'but we must know what you are doing at all times, as we could lose this contract.'

I was given cash, airline tickets, full itinerary, hotels, lunches; I did think it was very good. I dashed home to tell Betty that I had been chosen for this work. I told her that money was no problem and that if she needed cash at any time, just to ring Harry Cox and he would send her a cheque.

I flew to Ireland, arriving at Shannon Airport. The manager of the Irish airline was called English, and I soon got to know him better. I would say, 'Hello Irish English, how are you?' The airport staff were good to me, in fact I did not meet one Irish person who tried to shun me. I would say to anyone, if you want a good holiday go to Ireland, the punt (Irish currency) is like the £, no problem.

The next morning I was up early and waiting at the airport to meet the first group. The flight time from Chicago was about 8 hours, so they would be falling asleep by the time they arrived. Therefore, I just led them across the path to the hotel where I had all their room keys waiting for them, sat them in the lounge with a coffee and the hotel forms to complete and sign, and then sent them off to bed for a while.

After a good rest the group was up and ready to go. I ordered coffee to be served in a one of the large lounges, where I gave them a quick talk. 'Wherever you are ensure your pockets or bags with anything you treasure are kept an eye on at all times.' 'Try not to use the hotel phone to call home, here in

Ireland and the rest of the UK the phone box is much cheaper.' Also many other things of importance to them.

That evening we were off to Bunratty Castle to have a historical night, eating a meal with fingers and drinking mead as they did in the olden day. The evening entertainment would be old songs and everyone was dressed in olden day outfits. It was a good night's entertainment.

The next morning all were ready to start the tour. Our route took us into County Clare and up to Galway, where lunch was in the Great Southern Hotel. After lunch I gave them their room keys and then took them on an afternoon trip around Cornamona, where the top marble is made. The view here out to the Atlantic Ocean is a must, to see the sun drop down into the Ocean is tops.

The following morning we headed back towards Limerick and lunch in the George Hotel. It was full of church people, so I said to an Irish man, 'Is there a function going on?'

'No,' he said, 'it's like this all the time. Yet outside kids shake cans collecting money, with holes in their socks and short pants on, their families rely on the money that the kids can bring home.'

That night we were booked into another Great Southern Hotel, where we had dinner and then went to the local pub, called Conns. We had the best Irish welcome you could have, what a night! They sang loads of rebel songs, but I kept on singing 'There'll always be an England', I could not care less.

Next day we took the Ring of Kerry trip, which is again a must. They do say there that if you see 7 white horses you will end up having twins. We moved on to Cork and the Blarney Castle. To kiss the Blarney Stone we first had to climb to the stone at the top, then you have to lay on your back pulling yourself on a steel bar, and drop your head back over, tilting down a bit more to reach the stone to kiss it. The drop to the ground at this point was about 50 feet. Now I will probably have the Irish Tourist Board jumping up and down telling me that is not correct, perhaps it is only 48 feet, who knows?

After an overnight stop in Cork the next day we made our way to Wexford via Waterford, that is the place to buy your glass. If you go into Westminster Abbey look at the chandeliers hanging in the nave. The blue smoke of the glass is out of this world. The cost of each of these was £3000 to £4000 and was given to the Abbey in the year 1966. That is why I say to get your glass from Waterford.

Then it was on to the capital Dublin via Carlow. If you ever find yourself in that area do some fishing, the rivers are so full of salmon it's unbelievable. On arriving in Dublin I went into a bar. One thing about Ireland is that you can have a chat with someone without them thinking that you are on the tap for some cash, the people just make you feel good.

The next day was a trip around the City, seeing the Book of Kells; this is of the early Christian period, a great masterpiece. That night after dinner we went to the Abbey Theatre which was very good. From Dublin we went to Belfast, stopping at the Europa Hotel and the following day visited Parliament.

The flight from Belfast to Glasgow was funny, no sooner had you got up into the air than you seemed to be coming down again. It was only a short hop across the North Channel and the Firth of Clyde. I had problems but not on the flight, I just did not feel comfortable in Belfast, there was lots of talk, and I just heard about the Government amongst other things. The chat I heard was obviously the start of the trouble in Ireland. We arrived in Glasgow and took the main route to Edinburgh. However, driving through Glasgow, a football match had just finished and we were stuck in the middle of Glasgow Rangers and Celtic fans pushing the coach and making it sway from side to side. I opened the coach door and shouted out to them that this was a tourist party and that they were frightening my passengers, and so they let us proceed on our way.

Arriving in Edinburgh, the group was booked into the Caledonian Hotel, 5-star. In those days, if there were any passengers taking single rooms these were at the top and they had to walk down the corridor to the bathroom. I in fact called into the Caledonian last year and spoke to the under manager and asked him about the single rooms on the top floor. When I told him I had last visited 30 years ago he rolled up laughing and told me that it is not like that today. What I'm actually getting at is that in those days some of the passengers thought that I had one of the best room and many a time I would have to show them my room. The manager would tell them, 'Your guide pulls 2 desks together and then uses this mattress in the cupboard,' which he then showed to them, 'and he washes and shaves in this little sink or can take the lift to the top floor to the bathroom there.' That shut them up!

Edinburgh itself; the castle dominates the city centre, set astride the core of an extinct volcano. It's history dates back to the 6th century at the end of the Middle Ages when Edinburgh became Scotland's capital city. Today the Stone of Destiny is back in its rightful place in Scotland. The Royal Mile is a must along Princes' Street, and then to top it all we had the Robert Burns Night with the pipes and haggis (the national dish).

After a few nights in the city we made our way to England via Gretna Green. Again I entertained the group by marrying off different couples. Afterwards we had lunch in Carlisle and toured the northern part of the Lake District with an overnight stay in Keswick.

The following day we completed our tour of the Lakes and then made our way south to Liverpool to visit the new Cathedral, The Crown of Christ, or as the Liverpudlians called it 'Paddies Wigwam'. This was a new Cathedral built by Sir Edwin Lutyens and was completed in time for our visit. That evening we arrived in the city of Chester, again a must to visit the Tudor buildings at their best. Our 2 night stay was at the Grosvenor Hotel.

The next day we travelled along the top road to Wales, stopping at Holywell to visit a carpet factory. My passengers could not believe that the labour wages were £10 per week, this was 1967, and that was a weekly wage not daily.

We were near the place where St George fought the dragon, at a place called Bodelwyddan. If you ask the locals they will tell you it was at the Marble Church, built from white marble it can bee seen for miles. We had lunch at Llandudno then drove a different route back to Chester.

I will always remember my last tour for Cartan in 1969. We arrived back at the Grosvenor Hotel at about 6 pm and after taking a wash in my room I put on the TV and saw Astronaut Armstrong landing on the moon, the first man ever to do this.

Getting back to this tour, that night as we came back from north Wales, I said to the group, 'Tomorrow we leave at 8 am.'

'What for?' they asked.

'It's a secret.'

All night they would question me about where we were off to the next day to need to leave so early, but I wouldn't give in, just told them, 'You will love it.'

At 8 am the following day we moved off from Chester and drove to Staffordshire crossing over the main route. I asked them all to shut their eyes and then we drove to the Wedgwood factory. These people jumped for joy!

I told them, 'You are booked in for a tour which takes about an hour, but they will finish early for you so that you have time to shop. Do not worry about taking the purchases home on the coach, their export department will arrange everything for you.' For many years I had no problems with this, also remember that there was no tax to pay by having the goods shipped home.

We moved on to Coventry where lunch was at the Leofric Hotel. I got them to the hotel for 12.30 pm because at 1 pm the Lady Godiva clock moved and you could see the Peeping Tom as well. That would always go down well at lunchtime. We visited the Cathedral, the bombed and the new one. This city, along with many others, took a lot of bombing during the War.

Arriving at Stratford-upon-Avon at 5 pm, there was dinner and then rest until the next day.

A full tour of Stratford including Anne Hathaway's Cottage and Holy Trinity Church where Shakespeare's grave is towards the altar, and over to the left hand side near the altar steps, 13 feet down. On his gravestone reads a curse against anyone removing any of his bones. This is a place of God, so I asked for the church to be respected.

That evening there was early dinner followed by a visit to the Theatre. Although not one person ever told me they had not liked it, it is not like other theatres, in that the Shakespeare can be a bit rough on the ear.

Just a small note, if you are ever in Canada in the Toronto area, visit the Stratford Theatre there. It is the same as that in Warwickshire, but you should ring first to clear that the Theatre is open.

We departed Stratford and drove towards the Broadway which is a part of the Cotswolds, many of these towns and villages in the Cotswolds are what I chocolate box pictures. We went on to Oxford, again passing through Bladon to the church where Churchill and his parents were buried. Not far from there is Blenheim Palace where Churchill was born. After lunch we visited a college and then saw a lot of Oxford before we set off for London, arriving there at about 6 pm. I told them that the next day was a day of rest, so would see them the following day for a 9 am start. The day of rest meant I could spend a great day with my sons. However, do you remember I had the gambling bug? I ended up in the betting shop, what a *big nut* I was.

I did the London tour the way I like to do it; St Paul's Cathedral, Tower of London, then back for the Changing of the Guards outside Buckingham Palace, lunch, the WestEnd tour, Westminster Abbey, Bond Street and Oxford Street, Knightsbridge and the top shops.

The next day we were off again to Winchester and Salisbury Cathedrals. Winchester is where Jane Austin lies. Looking up at the stained glass windows, these were smashed by Cromwell's troops and were just replaced again without a pattern, this reminds us of the wrong things to do in the Cathedral of the Lord.

On to Salisbury where we had lunch in the Kings Arms, followed by the visit to the Cathedral with the 400 feet high spire. I told the group that the spire was perpendicularly out by 2 feet, and if they wanted to see this to follow me. I took off my coat and as we stepped into the cloisters I said again to look at it from a point across the yard, the whole group dashed over. By then I had thrown my coat over the sign that read 'Gentlemen's Toilet', and asked them to step into the spare tools department where they could look up and see the spire being out by 2 feet. I could hear some of the group stating that they could see this and others that they could not. By the time they had emerged from there I had put my coat back on and most of them realised that I had tricked them all along, they had just been in the Gents loo to look at a spire that was certainly not out in any way. This brought much laughter.

On the way back we stopped at Stonehenge to see the historic stones, and then talked about the stones on the journey back to London.

I got us back to London by 5 pm, some had bought Theatre tickets, so it was early dinner and then off to the Theatre. On the journey back from Stonehenge I talked about their departure from Heathrow Airport, and informed them that I would be there at the finish of their tour as well, to see them off safely.

I did these tours on and off for 2 years. During that time I was asked by the canteen staff at Shannon Airport to bring in contraception, and I did not charge them any more than what I had paid originally. This was a laugh! They would line up outside the canteen door for me, I did like my Irish friends, and if we can get on like this, what is the problem today?

Just before I finished my last Cartan tour, I was asked to go to America for a company called Alexandra Hamilton Life Insurance, to boost up their sales, and this I did. I went from

Boston to New York, stopping at Providence to do a live radio show. On the show the chap asked me what I thought of coffee. I told him, 'It's OK once you have chewed it.' That brought a lot of laughs. Then it was over to Detroit and Chicago and down to Indianapolis, and overnight in Evansville on the edge of Kentucky.

The trip was for 10 days, encouraging the sales staff to succeed and win their trip to England. The people were all very helpful. The news of the day whilst I was over there was of the death of Judy Garland in London and it was a great shock.

On my return to England, my Betty and the 2 boys met me at a London station. I had already completed my last trip with Cartan and it was now 1969.

One night I was sitting with Betty at home when there was a knock on the front door. It was Canon Collins who was also a music teacher. He told us that they would love to send Tony to Westminster Abbey to sing in the Abbey Choir. Well, I nearly fell off my chair. My boy Tony in the Abbey Choir? I laid down the law to him. As this would take place twice a week, school would let him off early, he was to have a light meal and drink then get the train to London. Walk the short walk to the Abbey and when the choir lesson was over, he was to wait for me. Nine times out of 10 I would already be there waiting for him, but if I wasn't he was to stay in the cloisters until I arrived. A thousand wild horses would not have stopped me from picking up Tony lad from the Abbey.

Then Betty and I received an invitation to be at Westminster Abbey to hear the choir singing 'The Messiah' by Handel. We were so pleased to be able to hear our lad sing and to see him dressed in his red and white outfit. When we got to the Abbey we were shown to our seats which were behind a Purbeck marble pillar in Poets Corner, and to top it all I was standing on top of the grave of Old Parr who died in 1635 at the ripe old age of 152.

In spite of all this, we enjoyed it and when it was finished Tony asked us, 'Did you see me?'

And we replied, 'Yes mate, and we are very proud of you.'

Tony sang at the Abbey for a long while after that. Even today singing is his hobby and he sings in Stratford in Toronto, Canada. Well done mate!

The trip to America did very well. We ended up with 3 planes full of the winners and the group was then split into 2. One group stayed at the Royal Gardens Hotel and the other at the Royal Lancaster Hotel, both near Kensington Palace and both hotels can be seen from the other across the park. The groups had already paid for the London tours and a half day trip to Windsor Castle, but we added optional trips to Stratford-upon-Avon and also Paris.

The Paris trip left at 5 am, the coach taking them to Manston Airfield on the south coast, the flight was 50 minutes to an airport near Paris. There they would be met by an English speaking driver and tour guide, see the sights of Paris, go shopping, followed by an early dinner at a club. Then back to the airport for the flight home, to be back in bed by midnight. I would say to them, 'Ladies, you will think you are Cinderella after this trip.' Mr Steve Feldon did the Paris side and I operated this side. The trip was on for every other day and the company did well.

When this tour left London, the family and I had a Fred Pontin holiday in Spain for 2 weeks. It was just what the doctor ordered, lots of rest and sunshine. However, on my return home I was informed that the bosses of the Victoria Sporting Club, for whom I was working, wanted me. Yes, they really did want me. Whilst I was away on holiday the big knives had been pushed in my back, Bernie had already gone, and the club offered me £500 to clear my desk and go. I did this, met up with Bernie, and then flew to America to tell the tour companies the truth behind what was going on. I asked if either Bernie or myself had let them down in any way, and the answer was 'no'. So we decided to take all the work away from the club, and the person who had stabbed us in the back would no longer benefit from it.

Bernie bought a company named Destination London and made me the Operations Manager. We had offices in Heron Court, Lancaster Gate, WC2 and still held on to the travel desk in the Royal Lancaster.

By now I was working full time for Bernie. We had large groups coming into London from New York, arriving on Friday morning and leaving on Sunday after lunch. The groups were big so we split them into 2 hotels, the Royal Lancaster and the London Hilton in Park Lane. We understood from the American office that the groups just wanted shopping and maybe a short tour of London, or a visit to the Theatre.

My staff had a travel desk by the back entrance, but we did not sell theatre tickets because the Hilton had its own travel desk. However, the group did come to us for information on this and that. The staff overheard the groups talking of the gambling clubs, and they helped them to find the best ones there were. After this happened for the third time, Bernie was called to the Home Secretary's office in Whitehall. He was told that all groups in future must sign in at a gambling club when first arriving in London and before going to their hotel. Then after 24 hours they could enter the club to gamble.

Bernie and I then sat down and worked out that we could run 2 coaches. The first to the Knightsbridge Club and when they had signed in take them to the London Hilton, which was close by. The second to the Victoria Sporting Club and when they had signed in take them just down Sussex Gardens to the Royal Lancaster Hotel.

I thought about it for a while then asked Bernie, 'Why can a person arrive at the airport, jump into a cab and ride into London, get out and walk into a betting shop and place a bet. What is the betting shop but a place to gamble, no different to a Casino which is a place to gamble? I cannot see what the Home Secretary is getting at.'

As time went on it was brought to our notice that there were names of the 'not wanted' in London – a Mafia outfit??

This was at the time when George Raft tried to buy a nightclub in Berkeley Square and he was stopped, and so left London. George Raft was the old time actor of the 40's to the 60's; he was good.

Whilst I am talking about Berkeley Square (pronounced Barclay), at number 45 lived Clive of India, a plaque is over the doorway. Then there was our Swedish Nightingale, Jenny Lind Goldschmidt, 1820 – 1887, who sang 'To hear a nightingale sing in Berkeley Square'. She lived at 189 Old Brompton Road and there is also a plaque for her at Westminster Abbey in Poet's corner.

We did a couple more groups like this and then they stopped coming to London. Was the Home Secretary right? Maybe!!

Whilst we had travel offices in the Royal Lancaster Hotel, we also had an operational office just around the corner from the hotel. The directors and myself were pleased with the set up, the Royal Lancaster was a 5-star hotel, and we had to ensure we were on the ball the whole time.

One day I received a phone call from the travel desk, and the young lady said, 'There are 2 gentlemen in the lobby who wish to speak to the Travel Desk Manager.'

I said, 'I'm on my way.'

On arriving at the hotel I met the 2 gentlemen and introduced myself. I offered coffee of which they declined, and indicated to seats in the lobby and sat down with them.

His Royal Highness Prince Faisal of Saudi Arabia had sent in these 2 gents, and the Prince was not happy about the Theatre tickets he had received from the hotel's travel desk. From the way these men spoke we could lose the account and then the hotel would blow a fuse – that means get very upset.

I said to them, 'Take my card and please ask His Royal Highness to call me if he likes what I am about to say. If he calls asking for seats in the first 2 rows from the front of the orchestra, I will drive to the theatre, pick up the tickets and deliver them in person. How about that for service?'

The 2 men smiled and said, 'We will go back and pass on the information.'

That afternoon I received a call and it was from His Royal Highness Prince Faisal. The Prince was over the moon that he could have his tickets collected and delivered to his door.

I was immediately on my way, calling out to Bernie on the way past, jumped into my small car and dashed to the West End to buy some theatre tickets. Then I drove back to an address in Mayfair, where I was escorted to a department and had the great honour of meeting His Royal Highness. I bowed, but the Prince said no, and held out his hand for me to shake; this was an honour.

This happened a few times, picking up and delivering the theatre tickets personally to the Prince. Then he said to me, 'What is your Christian name?'

'Harry,' I replied.

From then on His Royal Highness when speaking on the phone or in person referred to me as Harry.

I would like to say Prince Faisal is a fine gentleman and a nice guy.

Tony left school at 15 and his first job was working in a cable factory, but the manager was a bit rough with the lad. So like any Dad should do, I looked around Lancaster Gate and came up with a job at the Charles Dickens Hotel as a junior porter. But there was a problem; it was Tony's hair. I must say it was long at about 12 to 14 inches long, but it was the fashion of the day. Tony was told by his manager to have it cut, so he tried tucking it under his hat, but when he bent over to pick up the bags the hat would fall off.

One day the manager of the Royal Lancaster said to me, 'How is your Tony doing at the Charles Dickens?'

I told him, 'Very good, he is a hard worker just like his Dad.'

He then asked, 'Wages good, and tips?'

'Very good.'

He then told me, 'We can do better for him and more tips.'

That evening I put this to Tony, who said he would like to move to the big hotel, so I arranged a meeting for him with the manager of the hotel.

After the meeting I asked Tony how it had gone. 'Very good,' he said, 'but I must get a hair cut and then can start in 2 weeks time.'

I spoke to the manager at the Charles Dickens Hotel who was fine about the whole thing, and he even said that Tony was stepping up the ladder already. When Tony had his hair cut he looked completely different, just like he was when he was a choirboy at the Westminster Abbey.

I would go with him on the bus, route number 12 that I once drove, and if I got stuck at the airport he could then hop on a bus to Trafalgar Square. Then the Charing Cross train would take him home.

David, my other son, was still at the local Junior School, remember there is 7 years between the 2 of them. When I spoke to the Head Teacher about David, he told me that he was doing well and was very good in sport. I was pleased to hear that report.

For the year ending 1972 we had a party, the whole family was there, before I left work I told Bernie that I would be in on New Year's Day. By the time the party was slowing down in the early hours of the morning, I went to bed. However I did not go to my bedroom but into David's room where my Mum was fast asleep. We had 2 single beds in that little room and I climbed into the other one. Why, when my bed had Betty in it?

In the morning the phone rang, it was Bernie. I could hear Betty saying that I had already left for work, but I just felt that I did not want to go in to work. I just lay there looking up at the ceiling. There was to be a new coach waiting outside the Plaza Hotel at 10 am to take a group to Woburn Abbey in Bedfordshire. Most of London was closed for the day and I had arranged with Woburn Abbey for my coach to arrive about 12 noon to visit the Duke's home. But I was just lying looking at the cracks in the room's ceiling.

Another hour passed and the phone rang again. This time I dashed into my bedroom and picked up the extension phone. It was Bernie again.

'Sorry Bernie,' I said, 'but I am not coming to work today.'

'Why,' he asked.

'I don't know,' I replied, 'but I will see you tomorrow,' and put the phone down.

Betty asked me if I was OK, and I told her I was but just didn't want to go into work. I had a cup of tea and took one up to Mum. I asked her if she was OK and if she wanted some breakfast, to which she replied, 'Fine thanks love, but I'm all right with a nice cup of tea.'

It was lunchtime and Betty's brother Johnny and her dad went to the local pub called 'The Dukes Head', but I stayed at home with Betty, her Mum and my Mum. The boys were both out, Tony with his girlfriend and David playing.

The next hour was black.

I was looking out of the back windows and Mum was sitting in the front room, and Betty and her Mum were getting the food ready for lunch. I walked into the room with Mum and asked her if she wanted a drink.

'No thanks love,' she said, 'but I am not well, I just do not feel good.'

I quickly said, 'I'll call the doctor.'

'No, no, you don't need to do that,' Mum said. But I did and it was 1 pm.

We sat by Mum's side as she was saying, 'My Harry Boy has been good to me, and Betty has been good to me.'

I could feel the tears coming to my eyes.

Then Mum said, 'I cannot breath very good.' So like I did for my Dad, I grabbed a towel and started to fan Mum like a boxer, from side to side. By now I was jumping up and down waiting for the doctor to arrive, it was now 1.30 pm. I rang them again and was told he was on his way. Ten minutes later Mum said to me that she couldn't see, and then she just died whilst I held her hand. Then the doctor arrived, but it was too late. He told me that the local Coroner must be informed and that Mum would be taken to him within the next few hours.

We found out later that Mum had died of Bronchopneumonia, Chronic Cardiac Failure and Pleurisy. When I read this I could not believe it. Mum had not once said indoors that she was not feeling well until that Black Hour. What had made me stay at home and not go to work?

It felt just like the time in 1949 with Dad at the tram stop. We had hugged and I had tears in my eyes as I waved goodbye to him. That was the last time I saw Dad alive. Yes, I do believe there is a God.

On 8 January 1973 the whole family - cousins, aunts and everyone - turned up at Eltham Crematorium to see my Mum off and it was a grand send off.

I received a miserly £30 from an Assurance Company that Mum had been paying all her life, and another £30 from the Government, as in those days you did get that money, however the whole cost of the funeral was well over £600. The Funeral Director did a good job and I know my Mum would have been pleased with the way it went.

MY LAST STOP

I was still working for Bernie until I read an advertisement in the paper wanting a person to look after a depot in Crayford, and to write to the Chemicals Co for further information. And I did just that, with me living in Crayford it was right on my doorstep and could be the right move to make. Why did I want to leave Bernie? Well, the traffic was not so good any more, each year it was getting heavier, and the trains were murder. I would get on at Charing Cross Station and find there were no seats, then have to stand as far as Sidcup, and then once I had a seat it was only another 2 stations until Crayford. I would end up in pain all night and many a time I would end up going to work like that also.

I sent my response by Registered Post as it was Christmas time and I didn't want the letter to go astray. When I had my interview with Mr David Vigeon he told me that seeing my letter arrive by Registered Post made them sure this was the kind of person they were looking for. Someone who took care of even the small matters, in that I had ensured my letter reached them at such a busy time of the year.

I was given the job and started on 5 February 1975 reporting to Uxbridge, where I spent my first week in training. My overnight digs were at the Lex Hotel near Heathrow Airport, where you could sit and watch the flights arriving and taking off. I remember at the time on the TV was the news that Mrs Thatcher was taking the top dog position in the Conservative Party.

When I first looked at the depot in Crayford, I felt it was bloody rough. I was told by HQ that the stocks were down and absentees were high, but you could not blame the Under Manager, John, he was like a tiger with paper teeth. When I gave a talk to the whole staff, I told them that I would be watching them, and it may mean that some of them would end up leaving because I would be spot checking their loads leaving the depot. They would never know which truck would be checked, and I would ensure that no stock would leave the depot without a docket.

Two of the men watching at the time were Brian Hardy and Mick Seymour, both top workers. Brian had the long runs like Eastbourne, so I gave him the new truck and the other drivers went mad.

I said to them, 'OK, you do the long runs but try doing them with the old truck and see how many deliveries you can make in a day.' They didn't want to know.

The other lad, Mick was a bit more clever, he had a good head on him, and he came up with some good ideas about the stock in the depot.

Three months passed and the stock was getting better. I was jumping up and down on vehicles, checking their loads all the time. Giving the benefit of the doubt to a driver if I found some of the goods without dockets, but warning them that next time they would be asked to leave. I knew that people do make errors, so I did not want to start throwing my weight around unless it kept happening.

Stocktaking was always on a Friday and the store would be shut all day. I told them that was bonkers, with the amount of stock it shouldn't take more than 3 hours, but we would be there from 8 am to 11 pm.

I came up with a plan that we could do emergency runs to Gatwick airport, the Kent County schools, hospitals along with other customer, so the firm bought the depot a 1 ton van. The other trucks belonged to a hired truck garage and they would have their service done in Maidstone, Kent, but the drivers began bending my ears about the quality of the services we were getting. So I managed to move the service contract to a garage near Bermondsey, SE1, and got on well with the manager there. In fact I was invited to go to Football Club where they had a private box. I could have had all the drinks I wanted, but I had to turn this down for a cup of coffee as I was driving. This club lost on this occasion to Nottingham Forest 0-1.

In 1979 we moved to a brand new depot in Erith, Kent. This *was* going up in the world. I arranged the have the depot with the 45 gallon barrels along one side and all the dust bags near the large opening doors, this way no vehicle would be left outside. I would arrive at 6.30 am, start up the trucks and if one did not start I would call the fitter who lived in Plumstead and, at that time of the morning, he would be there in 20 minutes. That all started running smoothly. Then I took £35 out of petty cash and bought 6 inch spades for all the trucks and asked the drivers to keep them behind their co-driver's seat. Why did I buy these? The snows were beginning to get very heavy and I told the drivers, if they were stuck, use the spade to cut the bushes on the side of the road, clear the snow from under their wheels, stuff the branches under the wheels and that would get them moving. All the company trucks from Erith depot managed their deliveries, and the Manager at Uxbridge asked how we had managed this, we were the only depot still working.

A driver took his vehicle into the garage for a service and was told to return at 2 pm, which he did. On driving home down the Old Kent Road, he entered the one-way system at

New Cross and the engine blew up with a bang and stopped dead. The driver rang me and told me that the garage were coming to fetch the vehicle back ..

I said, 'Before they get to you check your dip stick and ring me back.'

About 5 minutes later he called and said, 'It's dry, no oil at all, that is why it went bang.' I said.

When it was returned to the garage, the manager spoke to me and said, 'Your driver should have checked the oil before setting off.'

I said, 'Come off it! Why did he bring it in, and what does he sign before taking out the vehicle? That it has been serviced. And service includes changing the oil.'

We found the young man who had worked on the truck and discovered that he had rushed off to a phone call. Chemicals Company did not push this any further.

My spare driver was Fred Potter; he worked in the depot when all the drivers turned up for work. One day the driver for East London did not show, so Fred went out at about 10 am. When Fred went out anywhere you would think he was off to the North Pole – maps everywhere – but he was such a nice guy to work with. At about 11.30 am I received a phone call from him saying he was not feeling well and had a pain in his chest.

I said to Fred, 'Do you want us to come and get you? Do you want to call the police to help you?'

Fred said, 'No, I will make it back to you.'

I repeated my words to him but again he said, 'No, I will be all right.'

Fred drove back into the depot at about 1 pm and I sent him straight off home with instructions to see his doctor immediately. That evening, Fred rang to tell me he was going into hospital the following day, and there he stayed for the next 6 weeks and off work for 6 months. He told me that his doctor had told him to thank his manager for making him go home. Remember what happened to me back in 1960? Not all people are skivers.

The company representatives were good. As they walked through the door their first word would be 'coffee'. Then we would talk about the business or the family. One of the reps was called Peter Trayling, and it was him who gave me the idea to write this book.

It was now 1982. One day I was taking my dog Spot for a walk to buy the morning paper and just stopped dead in my walk. The war injury that I had received whilst in Malaya in 1950 was giving me much pain. I phoned the War Benefit Department, told them of the problem, and an appointment was made for me with 2 doctors in Catford, SouthEast London.

The appointment was for 2 pm and the doctors finally arrived at 2.20 pm, and there were still lots of people waiting to see them after myself. One doctor shouted, 'Come in Mr Benton.' So I went into the room, sat down on the chair and told the 2 doctors about my injury. At that point they asked me to get up on the bed, and whilst I waited for them I removed my shoe and sock. The doctor pulled and tugged at my ankle and then told me that they could not see anything wrong with the ankle apart from the fact that it was swollen.

I said, 'How can you say that crap? Have you got x-ray eyes? Why do you not send me across the road to Lewisham Hospital for a x-ray?'

However, they were not prepared to do this and just told me that there was nothing wrong with my ankle, wrote their report and sent it back to the War Benefit Department.

About one week later it happened again, I just stopped dead in my walk. The pavement was full of people at the time all doing their shopping in Crayford, and when I just stopped they all bumped into me. So I sat on the kerb waiting for the pain to go away.

I went to see my doctor and said, 'If you do not help me, so help me God, I will cut off this ankle.'

He quickly said, 'No, do not do that, I will give you a note to go to Livingston Hospital.'

That afternoon I was there at the hospital, had the x-rays done, and a few days later a letter arrived calling me in to see Dr Seaton, a very nice guy. Dr Seaton told me that there was a foreign body floating around inside my ankle and now and again it was getting caught in my joint and causing the problem.

Two weeks later I met Mr Kamdar an Orthopaedic Doctor, and this great doctor did the job. Whilst in hospital I contacted the War Benefit Department and told them to make the 2 doctors from Catford aware.

I have been under the knife by Mr Kamdar many times now. If you could see it now, there's not much left of an ankle, just a bit of bone here and there. I am currently under 2 hospitals; the Medway Disabled Service Men and also Gravesend Hospital, the Trauma and Orthopaedics Department. From my knee to my toes all that I can move are my toes, the rest of my leg is like a block.

My eldest son Tony met a young Irish lass whilst on holiday in Greece, her name was Jackie. My phone bill ended up being very high, so I told Tony only to phone her at weekends, but he didn't listen and the bill continued to get higher.

Romance bloomed and they married in Dublin in 1982. A week earlier in London we had had a visit from the IRA, do you remember it? The bandstand in Regents Park along with the Royal Horse Guards were blown up, troopers and horses, just as they reached Hyde Park Corner.

Back to the wedding. We arrived at Gatwick Airport, all our bags were double-checked by the police, and then we had a good flight over. Tony met us at the airport and we went off to meet Jackie's family. We had a cup of tea and a chat and then went to leave saying we would see them the next day at the Cathedral in Dublin. Tony decided we were going to the airport bar for a drink and the whole family ended up there. I said, 'This is a funny looking Cathedral,' it was a good night.

The wedding went very well and I was so pleased for him, he is a Benton, part of a family of very hard workers like so many other families.

On 3 June 1983 I came home and the car was parked outside our house. Thinking Betty was home early I called out to her, but there was no answer. I called again, but still nothing. Then I saw it; a letter 13 pages long, which read that Betty had left me. I broke down and when David came home we both just sat there crying. The phone rang and it was Betty, she was crying also, but she asked me not to try to see her at her place of work and make trouble for her, I said I wouldn't and I kept my word. David at first did not want to speak to her until I said to him, 'Come on mate, this is your Mum. For my sake please talk to her,' and he did.

We were divorced in August that same year, however we do still speak to one another from time to time. Tony got a divorce also and is now remarried with a young son, Richard, who is 9 years old. Tony is a Registered Massage Therapist in Stratford, Ontario in Canada. Good on you son!

David was doing very well working at a bakery during the school holidays, for which he earned £45 a week. He also joined the bakery's football team; he got on well with people. When he left school he worked for the bakery for 5 years, they were good to him and started his training in engineering. After that he got a job in the City as he was able to earn much more money, and he would have weekends off.

One good thing that *I* managed to accomplish was to stop the gambling. How did I do this after all those years of wasting my money? Of chasing the invisible Midas touch, the ability to make money? When I would pass a betting shop I would cover my ears. If I bumped into a friend in the street who started talking about a dog or horse race, I would say, 'Sorry, I have just remembered, I have left a pot on the stove,' or words to that effect that would move me on without seeming too rude. I did not buy a newspaper for a whole year and if the staff began talking about sport I would leave the room. My football team, Crystal Palace, may have lost all their games; I did not want to know. But I did it. I stopped the gambling.

During 1984 I had a few visits from the Area Manager, there was no change in the manner of his talk, it was just the same as it had always been. We went to lunch at the local pub just as we had always done. A week later details of the wages' increase for all came through, marked for my attention only. All the staff were to get a rise of 4%, but yours truly only had 1%. Before I started jumping on someone's head, I rang Mary Innes, the lady who did the wages.

Mary said, 'Sorry Harry, but it is right. You only have a 1% rise.'

I rang the Area Manager and said, 'Are you taking the p***, what is all this rubbish of just 1%?'

He told me that he had tried to get my rise higher, but that the directors would not budge.

I then sent a telex to the MD asking what was going on, but did not receive an answer back. I spent some time doing deep thinking about the whole matter, and finally decided to change my position and go into sales. I had already been there for 10 years and received my watch, so I gave in my notice and said I would like to go on the sales side of the company.

A month later I was on the training course for salesmen at the Coventry Plant. A large meeting, open to anyone, was being held at this depot at 2 pm in the Company Restaurant. Now, hold on to your hat, I then saw the dirtiest trick I have ever heard about or seen. Why did I only get 1%? I worked really hard on my job, starting work at 6.30 am, checking the trucks to ensure they started, the depot had the top stocks in the country, and I trained other managers for other depots. The MD was running the meeting himself and now you will learn as to why I was just getting the 1% increase.

The MD stated that the Directors had decided to close all the depots in the county and the Coventry depot would be used for production and all deliveries, we would cover the whole of the UK.

I was dumbfounded, and a little bird said, 'Harry mate, that is why you only received a rise of 1%, so that you would leave and lose your redundancy money.

I rushed to the phone and spoke to Mary Innes asking her, 'Mary, what have I lost?'

She replied, 'I am very sorry Harry, but I have only just received the word on the company. Harry, you have lost £7500 in payment.'

I was fuming and I saw that p*** of a Manager, and he could see that I was very upset with the way the company worked. However, I had my new position, I got on with it and boy, did I work hard.

At first I was given Essex but only for a short time, just 2 months. Then I was handed Kent, so I moved to put myself in the centre of a wheel or the bull's eye on a dartboard. Kent's monthly income was only £4 or £5 thousand a month. Within 4 months I had added another 3 grand, and within 6 months a further 2 grand, I in fact doubled their sales, and it did say so in the Company magazine.

If I had to go to Coventry I would not speak to the Manager or Directors, as I would only have told them what I thought of them. If one of them said, 'You are doing well Harry,' I would just nod and walk on.

In 1990 I saw Mr Kamdar, my old bone man and he said to me, 'What year did you start work Mr Benton.' I told him it was in 1945 when the war was still on. He told me that I should pack up the work now as I had done my stint. So on 4 December 1990 I stopped work. Why? Many places I visited for sales, I would go into a kitchen, and the drum (25 litres) would be empty and needed changing. This I did but today I must check carefully. Weight lifting did my ankle no good.

Well, that's the end of my story. There's an awful lot more that I could have included, but I've tried to keep it interesting but short. You never know, when I reach 80 I could be writing the second edition!

b)

c)

d)

e)

POST OFFICE

TELEGRAM

Charges to pay

s. d.

RECEIVED

Prefix. Time handed in. Office of Origin and Service Instructions. Words.

From

TS2001 6030 3.36 PROSPECT KT 21

67

No.

At

To

By

HENRY BENTON 14 GOLDWELL HOUSE EAST-DULWICH-SE22 =

: TOP DECK SHOWING TONIGHT NATIONAL FILM THEATRE

AT 6.15 AND 6.30 RING ANDREWS PROSPECT 5242 +

14 SE22 6.15 6.30 5242 + TS 2001 +

h)

i)

The Courtesies

OF THE

POLICE DEPARTMENT

ARE EXTENDED TO

Mr. Harry Benton

BY THE

CITY OF MIAMI BEACH FLORIDA

Jay Dermer

JAY DERMER, MAYOR

j)

INDEX